KINGDOM of LIGHT II

kingdom of Darkness

Spiritual Warfare and The Church

For

God the Father

God the Son

And God the Holy Spirit

Endorsements

"It is an awesome responsibility to be able to rightly understand and share the Word of God. The Holy Spirit makes this possible but it takes maturity and study as well. Michael Hicks is a gifted teacher of the Christian faith.

"It has been a deep blessing to get to know Michael. His faith, integrity and honesty have helped many a seeker of the Good News of the Gospel come into the Church. People who know him are drawn to him because they see the presence of God in how he lives. There is no question about Jesus being the Lord of his life.

"His books show the years of research and study that have gone into them. His language is simple to understand. His thoughts are clear and scriptural. It has been a joy to know Michael and it has been a blessing to have had him as part of my life."

Pastor Duane Baker

"Minister Michael Hicks is a true inspiration. Kingdom of Light – kingdom of Darkness is a reality check for any reader. There are not many ministers speaking the unadulterated truth for fear of not pleasing the itch of the receiver, Minister Mike has not held back in speaking the truth. I look forward to future writings and encourage everyone to follow his teachings as it is clear that God is using him to be a voice in the twenty-first century."

Pastor Travis Hollon
Pastor emeritus Full Gospel Believers

"I have known Minister Michael for almost seventeen years and he has been an inspiration to me and many others over the years. He has great insight of the spiritual battles we face each and every day. Minister Mike's Kingdom of Light – kingdom of Darkness series is a must read for believers and even non-believers. It will help prepare us for the battles we will face each and every day of our lives."

Minister Garold Butler
V.B.C. Facilitator

"Michael Hicks does a great job explaining the plans of the enemy of man, Satan, and our power to defeat him. His explanation of

Endorsements

Scripture to guide us to victory is both thorough and easy to grasp. This is a must read for new believers and an excellent discipleship tool for the Christian education instructor."

Deacon Michael Norton, Teacher
Total Christian Life Ministry
Joliet, Ill.

"I was greatly blessed by Minister's Hicks' book, Kingdom of Light – kingdom of darkness in which the Holy Spirit spoke to my spirit."
Pastor Paul Revels

"Kingdom of Light – kingdom of Darkness is insightful and inspirational. A must read for all believers in Christ. It is a blueprint into fighting the spiritual fight of faith. I love the way Pastor Mike has broken down the word so even the newest of believers can understand how to have the wisdom to apply the Word of God and to win supernatural battles that we as believers face every day."
Pastor James Back
Christ Church United

"Michael has a unique way of breaking down the Scriptures where new creatures in Christ can understand their new life and position in Christ. His insight has helped many understand what it means to be a true Christian and the plans of God as a true Christian. This series is a must read for the young and old in the Body of Christ."
Sonja L. Hicks
First Lady YAH Jireh Ministries

"It is such a great honor for me to write this forward for this anointed series on spiritual warfare. Personally, Minister Mike clarified some things I've been going through and I am sure others are also. This series is very unique and is surely a work to treasure for anyone for reads and studies the Bible. Thank you so much Mike for producing such a masterpiece."
Evangelist Tajuana "Tee" Brown
Church of the Living God Temple 290

KINGDOM of LIGHT II

kingdom of Darkness

Spiritual Warfare and The Church

by Minister Michael R. Hicks

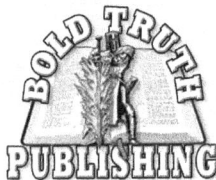

BOLD TRUTH PUBLISHING

Christian Literature & Artwork
A BOLD TRUTH Publication

KINGDOM of LIGHT II kingdom of Darkness
Copyright © 2017 by Michael R. Hicks
ISBN 13: 978-0-9981531-3-1

Printed in the United States of America

Bold Truth Publishing
300 West 41st
Sand Springs, Oklahoma 74063
www.BoldTruthPublishing.com

Table of Contents

Table of Contents

Table of Contents

Table of Contents

Table of Contents

Prelude

There is no doubt about it; the United States of America is spiraling down the wrong direction. She is slipping into darkness. The freedom we enjoyed as a nation has led us into moral decay, bad decisions, greed, pride and the final nail in the coffin may be the legalization of gay marriages which is an abomination to Jehovah. Homosexuality is not the only abomination unto God, there's pagan worship to false gods, child sacrifices, idolatry, Spiritism, and heathen practices in the House of God, just to name a few. Acts of abominations have an effect on the communities and the nation itself; it also leads to civil unrest in which deceit, murders, and destruction are common occurrences. When civil unrest persists, it leads to chaos and chaos will lead to civil war and possible annihilation. We have gone from one nation under God to one nation under multiple gods.

The Pilgrims were a group of roughly 100 people who sailed from England to the United States of America, then known as the New World to escape religious oppression. The Pilgrims came to the New World to worship God without the traditions of men and state sanctioned rituals force on them by the Church of England.

Throughout the centuries, many people from many nations have also came for religious freedom and the freedom to live their lives as they wished. The only problem with these nations, tribes and tongues is they brought their own gods with them and evangelized their doctrine/Gospel from coast to coast. The gods, led by Satan have influenced this nation to the brink of spiritual and moral decay. Slogans such as, "it's your thang – do what you want to do," and "Be yourself," and "I am free to do what I want to do," has hypnotized the nations into a Godless way of life. This last presidential election displays evidence of how far we, as a nation, have separated ourselves from the True and Living God.

In Kingdom of Light – kingdom of Darkness, Part One, we went over the cause of the world's present condition and the author of our fall. We looked at Satan's plan for man and his tactics to bring every male and female to share in his death sentence. We discussed his ability to transform into an angel of light to commandeer as many human beings into worshipping false religions, adhering to false Messiahs and a living lives of revelry, sexual immorality, heresies, adultery, idol worship, jealousies, murders, thief, outburst of wrath, drunkenness, sorcery, lewdness, selfish ambitions, dissensions, and uncleanness. These practices are alive and well and are proficient in the lives of lost Americans from coast to coast.

Satan is still holding a grudge against God for exposing his thoughts of greatness and prominence. He knows he can't defeat God so he goes after His children, His creation to deceive as many as he can to hurt Him. From the Garden of Eden through now, he has been winning souls by the millions into his rebellious camp against God. His most successful gift is causing the Bible; God's Word, to be of no effect for the people of the earth through deceit, confusion, and lies. Free choice can be great or it can be disastrous, depending on the decisions we make.

In Kingdom of Light – kingdom of Darkness, Part Two, we will look at God the Father, God the Son and God the Holy Spirit. We will also look at the function of the Church and leaders of the Church. We as the body of Christ need to get back to the basics of our worship and service to the Lord. Our lives depend on it.

Foreword

As the years go by, we as a people are floating *away* from God. From Kings and Palaces to Prime Minister's offices and the White House, we as a people are falling away from **THE TRUTH OF GOD**. We as a people are *straying* from the concepts that God has laid out for us to be successful in life. We, as a people are adopting *lifestyles, ideas,* and *realities* that cause nations to *fall,* when other empires have fallen in the past from the exact same practices. And as we continue to *compromise* against the Word of God and the teachings of Christ Jesus; we too will fall.

This book is not meant to bash any people, religion or lifestyle but to simply tell **THE TRUTH** according to the Word of God. Many people have been *snared* by the *tricks, skits* and *shenanigans* of Satan and have *grown comfortable* in his *"live free"* from the ideals, nature and doctrine of the Kingdom of Light – his *anti*-God doctrine. This freedom will *cost us* our lives and most importantly, will cost us eternal life.

The True and Living God is a good God and He wants us to be successful in our lives upon the earth, but when we *run away* from home, *away from* the doctrine of life, we become *aliens* to the His Kingdom.

My prayer is to find our way back to God.

Michael Ray Hicks

Acknowledgments

I would like to dedicate this book
to the following people for their support:

Sonja Hicks,
Wilmer and Queen Hicks,
Doctor Mark A. Hick,
Mitch Mullen,
Brother Vince,
Duane Baker,
Jerome and Jackie Gates,
Jack Hawkins,
Mr. and Mrs. Paschal Thompson,
Open Skies Ministry,
Billy Joe and Sharon Daugherty,
Kenneth Hagin Sr.,
James Slim Crabtree,
John and Melissa Barrett,
Common Ground,
Promise Keepers,
Rhema Ministries,
Willie James and Pamela Hankerson,
Michael and Renee Norton,
Leoddis Clay,
Don Bowers,
Brian Wideman,
Tony Mac,
Gary and Sally Wisenbach,
Steve Young,
Dr. Coyette Morgan,
The Fire Ladies,
Brother Daryl Holloman,
Mike and Carol Moody,
Dove Christian Fellowship,
Robert McGown,
Truckers for Christ,
Alonzo and Marvinette Ponder,
Glenda Bishop,
Ron Qualls,
Bill Boyd,
Bob Jones,
The Full Gospel Believers
and The Body of Jesus Christ
Community Church

Prayer

Most gracious Heavenly Father
I thank You and I give You praise –
for You are God and God alone
I thank You for Your Grace and mercy that held me
Through the years
I thank You for Your salvation that changed my life forever
I thank You for the work that You have given me to do
I thank You for the ones who will read this book
And get an understanding of the spiritual warfare
That everyone is involved in
And I pray that we all get revelation knowledge
On who we are in Christ
And revelation knowledge that we are
In Christ Jesus
That we are the head and not the tail
That greater are You that lives in us than
the devil that is in the world
Speak to our hearts and reveal Yourself to us all
In Jesus name,
Amen

Notes:

Chapter 1

God's Doctrine

The Bible

All Scripture originates from the mind of God and is spoken or written for instruction, history and spiritual intent for every human being on the face of the earth. Scripture is the pure truth of God's sacred thoughts, ideas and realities, and for centuries He has declared, shared, and foretold every event that has taken place, is taking place now and events that will take place in the future. The Scriptures are the epitome of His truth and the embodiment of His nature, His character, and His being.

There are millions who have read the collection of Scriptures named the Bible but only a few can truly read or understand it. In order to understand the Bible, you have to be initiated by the Spirit of God (Born-again). If you are not initiated by the Holy Spirit, you will not understand the message of God clearly. Carnal and natural man cannot understand the nature of God and their attempt to understand the Scriptures without the leading of God the Holy Spirit is disastrous. Without God's guidance it leads men and women into heresies', false doctrines, rebellion, spiritual blindness, and eventually the lake of fire. When we look back into history, we can see the difference between real men of God and people who claimed to be men of God.

The Scriptures tell the story of creation, the devil, the fall of man, God's love and dealings with men, the first coming of Jesus, the gift of salvation, the character and conduct of the Church, and the events before the second coming of Christ, the return of Christ and eternal life.

2 Timothy 3:16-17

All Scripture is given by inspiration of God, and is profitable for doctrine, for reproof, for correction, for instruction in righteousness, that the man of God may be complete, thoroughly equipped for every good work.

Every scripture is given by the inspiration of God. This means that every scripture is the truth because it originated from The Truth. Remember, God cannot lie. The Bible is the authentic Word of God, it is dependable, reliable, genuine, and accurate and we should respect it as so. We live by faith in His Word and not by our understanding.

The Scriptures describe God, His dominance, His love for His creation, belief systems, the plan of salvation and the recipe for eternal life. God gives us instruction but it is up to us to obey the Word of God. Sometimes people obey the Word and sometimes they don't. There are rewards for those who obey and consequences for those who don't. Every person that has lived, is living, and those to come will fulfill one Scripture or another? One group of people will fulfill – "Well done thy good and faithful servant" while others will fulfill "get away from Me you workers of iniquity." The Scriptures you fulfill in your life are up to you.

All Scripture is profitable for doctrine.

All Scripture is God breathed. All the writers of the Bible simply took dictation from the Spirit of God, for God is truly the author of the Bible. Men of God wrote what He said in every verse, paragraph, chapter, and book. God did not make any mistakes, errors, or inaccuracies while He dictated His Word to His Prophets.

All Scripture is helpful, informative, enlightening, supportive, edifying, and educational in the doctrine/teaching of God. God gave Scripture so that we may understand, and comprehend His story and His intentions toward the human race. The Scriptures are the blueprints of life for instructions, for history, for today, and the days to come.

The doctrine of God is simply God's teaching. It is a policy, a guideline, a principle, a creed, or a code to Godly living. When God sent Jesus to earth to redeem mankind, He taught the realities of the Kingdom of God. He taught what happens when we believe and follow His Father's Word and He also warned us what would happen when we disbelieve the Word of God. In this we are taught, and instructed how to act, how to live and who we should believe in.

There are many doctrines in the world and there are many religions and a diversity of people in the world. But there is only one true doctrine which is the doctrine/teachings of Jesus Christ. It is a principle, a body, or a collection of principles presented for acceptance in belief. The doctrine of Christ is found in *The Gospels of Matthew, Mark, Luke,* and *John.*

There are some groups of people around the world who believe men took God's Word and changed what God inspired. Some believe that God does not mean what He says in His Word. To this I say, "God is well able to protect His Word. He is well able to keep His Word." If men can overcome God and change His Word then God would not be much of a God. If all the minds that ever lived got together and formed into one – they're thoughts would still be smaller, minor, insignificant, and just plain trivial compared to the thoughts of God. His ways are significantly higher than anything we can imagine.

For Reproof

In Strong's Exhaustive Concordance, Greek #1649 and #1650, the word *reproof* is a conviction, or a rebuke. An example of this is found in *The Book of Galatians 2:11.*

Galatians 2:11
Now when Peter had come to Antioch, I withstood him to his face, because he was to be blamed; for certain men came from James, he would eat with the Gentiles; but when they came, he withdrew and separated himself, fearing those of the circumcision. And the rest of the Jews played the hypocrite with him, so that even Barnabas was carried away with their hypocrisy.

Now remember, Peter had a vision while he was praying upon the roof of Simon's house; the vision pertained to Gentiles receiving the salvation of Jesus Christ. When he received the vision, he went to Cornelius' house and gave a history lesson about: *"How God anointed Jesus of Nazareth with the Holy Spirit and with power, who went about doing good and healing all who were oppressed by the devil, for God was with Him."*

The veil of the temple was 4 inches thick, and sixty feet in length, the width was thirty feet and it weighed four tons, and it took three hundred men to hold it. This veil was torn in two which separated the Holy place from the Most Holy Place. When the veil in the Temple was torn from top to bottom; God gave access for everyone to come to Him through His Son. The tearing of the veil denotes that Gentiles now have the ability to become sons of God. It was no longer a Jewish thing, but a whosoever thing and one of the signs in which we gain access to God by Christ Jesus.

The Law was fulfilled and the liberty of Christ is presented to every tribe, tongue and nation. The world now has the ability to choose Jesus as Lord and Savior. Jesus put an end to all sacrifices and ceremonial activities to please the Lord. Everything changed in service to God from outer works to faith in Christ Jesus.

Well, Peter and the Gentiles were getting along very well, eating together and fellowshiping together. But when certain men came from James, (the Pastor of Jerusalem Church) he withdrew and separated himself from the Gentiles. Why did this happen? Around this time there were some Jews that wanted the Gentiles who believed in Christ to be circumcised and to observe the law.

Peter had a moment. He became fearful because he did not want to be seen eating and fellowshiping with the Gentiles. He did not want to be seen living in the liberty of Christ Jesus for fear of retaliation. And for this reason, Paul rebuked, withstood or convicted Peter to his face, stating that if the natural born Jews could not keep the law, why force the Gentiles to keep the Law.

Going back to the law is like taking a pig out of the muck, mud and mire and putting it into a bathtub. The pig is washed with soap, oiled down and released. After a while, the pig returns to the pig-pen, back into the muck, back into the mire, back into the mud and feces the pig has known all his life. It is all the pig knew, and all he expected in his life.

The Jews were in the same line of thinking, they attempted to live by the law because it was all they knew. They hung their hopes on Moses who prophesied about Christ but they missed it. By law Peter couldn't enter the house of any Gentile, he certainly couldn't dine with one or have any dealings with any Gentile. Peter didn't know if these Jews would stone him to death for mixing with the Gentiles and became fearful.

There are many churches in the world today that tries to mix the Law of Moses with the Grace of Christ. We cannot be successful as a body of Christ trying to work the Law while living in the grace of our Lord and Savior Jesus Christ. In fact, when we hold the traditions of the Law or men, we handcuff the power of God in our lives and in our church. It's like spiritual schizophrenia when we attempt to live by works and call it living by grace.

In *John 16*, Jesus gave His disciples some last minute information on the Kingdom and about the Holy Spirit;

> *John 16:7-8*
> *Nevertheless I tell you the truth. It is to your advantage that I go away; for if I do not go away, the Helper will not come to you; but if I depart, I will send Him to you. And when He comes, He will convict the world of sin, and of righteousness, and of judgement.*

Jesus told His disciples when the Holy Spirit comes He would convict the world of sin due of unbelief in Christ Jesus. The world would be convicted of righteousness because Jesus was going back to the Father and of judgment because the ruler of this world (Satan) has been judged and found guilty for leading the rebellion against The Holy One.

The world or society's way of doing things is the example of sin. The decisions of the world are born from flesh, or carnal thinking.

5

They are made without seeking the knowledge or the wisdom of God. Life without God is a sin and you cannot have God without Jesus.

Romans 8:5a
For those who live according to the flesh set their minds on the things of the flesh,

This is why the world we live in is so tragic. Law makers and high ranking leaders have forsaken God and made decisions based on money, prestige, power, and the pleasing of men. There are so many anti-God organizations born of Satan and carried out by the flesh of men; it is a wonder we are still here. Jesus calls this era, the beginning of sorrows.

The Holy Spirit will convict the world of sin. Christians should not focus on sins, but on Jesus. We should focus on what Jesus did for humanity when He died on the cross for the sins of us all. When He shed His blood on the cross, it was a full pardon for us and the only cure for our disease of sins.

The Holy Spirit will convict the world of righteousness. The work of Jesus Christ dying on the cross for our sins was completely righteous. When God the Father raised Him from the dead, it shows and signifies His approval of the righteous payment and His acceptance of Christ into His presence.

The Holy Spirit convicts the world of the nature of righteousness; remember our self-righteousness is compared to as filthy rags which are used kotex or tampons. The Holy Spirit shows us true righteousness as a gift from God to those who are in Christ. The Bible reveals we are the righteousness of God in Christ Jesus. We as children of God have been made righteous so that we have right standing with God.

The Holy Spirit will convict and judge Satan for he is the ruler of this world. He rules the hearts of the carnal, the fleshly, the erotic, the lascivious, the sensuous, and the unregenerate and leads them in blindness, willful rebellion, ignorance, disobedience, and spiritual error. Satan was judged at the cross, and all who follow him, agree with him, serve him and deceive the world with him are already judged with him.

6

For Correction

There will be times when we make mistakes as a person even if we are Christians. We have a lot against us in the world, but Jesus tells us that even though we are in the world, we are not of the world. The world does not like correction, but we as sons and daughters of God should welcome correction, especially when it comes from the Holy Spirit. In the world we will make mistakes as Peter did earlier in this chapter. Thank God for the Holy Spirit who corrects us when we get off track!

I heard a parable of a man that was in the fires of hell running around lifting the heads of men and women who also been sentenced to the lake of fire and brimstone. He lifted the head of one man and he responded, "Who are you looking for?" The man retorted, "I'm looking for that preacher who lied to me."

There are a lot of Bishops, Pastors, Teachers, and Evangelists who need correction according to the Scriptures because they are not holding true to the Word of God. The kingdom of Darkness has desensitized many churches that started with faith based teachings but their faith shifted to serve another Jesus the Bible doesn't recognize. Also the qualifications for leadership listed in Timothy and Titus have been overlooked or just ignored which opened the door for the devil to introduce and teach and preach a different Gospel.

There are some ministers that don't want to hurt anyone's feelings and will preach the common feel good sermon that won't offend anyone. However, they do not know they are offending God by not speaking His Word for the occasion. There are some preachers of churches who have a weekly program, itinerary, or schedule and will not adhere to the promptings of the Holy Spirit to change the message. Then there are some Preachers/Teachers who do not seek God for their sermons. But they will download someone else's sermon from the internet, I call it "Dial a sermon". It is really a scary thing to see because Paul wrote to Timothy almost two thousand years ago that in these last days people will not heed sound doctrine, will not heed correction and will hire teachers that would tell them what they want to hear instead of what they need to hear.

Jesus came down from Heaven not only to save us from our sins, but also to correct us when we make mistakes. We were born sinners and all our lives we lived in sin, we lavished in sin until we gave our lives to Christ. When we were born-again, only our spirit was saved. Our mind, will, and emotions were not saved and we found ourselves in a new battle – the battle between the flesh and the spirit. As we make the transition from fleshly to spiritual, (renewing our minds and obedience to His Word) we will make mistakes and with mistakes come correction.

Jesus did a lot of correction with the Pharisees, Sadducees, and Scribes. Their interpretation of the Law had drifted into darkness and they had no clue they were lost in the darkness. Jesus also had to correct Peter because he also did not have a clue,

> *Matthew 16:21- 23*
> *From that time Jesus began to show to His disciples that He must go to Jerusalem, and suffer many things from the elders and chief priest and scribes, and be killed, and be raised on the third day. Then Peter took Him aside and began to rebuke Him saying, "Far be it from You Lord; this shall not happen to You!"But He turned and said to Peter, "Get behind me Satan! You are an offense to Me, for you are not mindful of the things of God, but of the things of men."*

This is a strong rebuke or correction for Peter, for he, like the Pharisees, Sadducees, and scribes were off the mark concerning spiritual matters. Peter said that because He believed Jesus to be invincible, unconquerable, and insuperable because He is the Son of God; he further believed that no man or group of people could ever overcome Him. Now the Holy Spirit revealed to Peter that Jesus is the Son of the True and Living God, but that was all He revealed at that time.

When Peter heard the Master saying, *"He must go to Jerusalem, and suffer many things from the elders and chief priest and scribes, and be killed, and be raised on the third day."* Peter's mind went into a protective mode and he wanted to protect the Son of God and correct His view on future events.

When Jesus retorted, *"Get behind Me Satan!"* He scolded, rebuked or corrected him because his thinking was not in the plans of God for Jesus. To Jesus, Peter was off course and his thinking and was aligned with the thinking of Satan. If Jesus didn't die on the cross, the world would continue to be living in sin.

> *1 Corinthians 2:6-8*
> *However, we speak wisdom among those who are mature, yet not the wisdom of this age, nor the rulers of this age, who are coming to nothing. But we speak the wisdom of God in a mystery, the hidden wisdom of God which God ordained before the ages of our glory, which none of the rulers of this age knew; for had they known, they never would have crucified the Lord of glory.*

The principalities, the powers, the rulers of darkness of this age, and spiritual host of wickedness in heavenly places did not know the plan of God for Jesus. This evil spiritual government that was guiding the Pharisees, Sadducees, the Sanhedrin, the chief priests and the scribes were ignorant of God's plan for Jesus the Messiah. They did not know when Jesus died; God would raise Him up after three days even though this plan had been prophesied for approximately four thousand years. They did not know that believers would be empowered with the Holy Spirit to live free from the demons, devils, and evil spiritual rulers. Had they known, they would not have crucified our Lord; but they would have done whatever it took to keep Jesus safe from the elders and chief priest and scribes in order to keep the world in darkness.

All believers still need correction today. There will be times when we come across a Scripture that we cannot comprehend. When we do, we should pray about it and be still. When we take off and try to preach or teach a Scripture we don't fully understand, then we'll be in the same position Peter was when Jesus corrected him. The churches that fit this description need to repent and realign ourselves with the entire Gospel of Christ.

9

For instruction in righteousness

Instructions refer to the process of growing up spiritually. When we give our lives to Christ, we began the process of learning of Him. We start as babes in Christ and the more we learn of Him the more we grow in Him. These are the basic principles of the oracles of God which are listed in *Hebrews 5:*

The foundation of repentance from dead works and of faith toward God.

The foundation of repentance is a sorrowful heart. We have lived our lives in violation of God's purpose and God's truth. When we come to Christ, our eyes are opened and we are able to see we have to change our lives. Repentance from dead works is a change of heart or a change of mind about the demands of the Law of Moses. Even though the Law was good, it was weak because of our sin nature. The darkness had a hook in our jaw and we really had no choice but to sin. However, that condition changed through Jesus Christ's death, burial and resurrection in which we can truly have faith in God.

There are many churches today living under The Law and also trying to live under God's grace at the same time. These are dead works. This will never be accomplished; it is like a grape vine attempting to produce peaches or a watermelon vine attempting to produce apples. The Law and Grace are on opposite sides of the spectrum because the Law produces death while Grace produces life. Gentiles (Black people, White people, Indians, Mexicans, Chinese, Koreans, Japanese and all other races), were never under The Law; we were a law of our own. But there are some churches preaching a law that does not have any value in Christian living. In order to live under The Law, we would have to keep every jot and title in the Law. We would have to sacrifice bulls and goats and keep all the ceremonial practices and then some. Jesus fulfilled the Law when He died for our sins and now we are under the Law of Grace, which is God's divine influence upon the hearts of men. Why would anyone sign up to live in the Law of Moses, producing dead works for dead people and forsake the grace of God. Don't you know that when you live under the law, you are covered with a veil and will not be able to comprehend anything that pertains to spiritual matters? This veil can only be removed with the revelation of Jesus Christ.

Some people will ask, "What about the Ten Commandments?" The Ten Commandments have not been done away with – they have been simplified.

> *Matthew 22:37-39*
> *You shall love the Lord your God with all your heart, with all your soul, and with all your mind. And the second is like it: You shall love your neighbor as yourself.*

The Ten Commandments are summed up in the above Scripture. When we live by this, we are fulfilling the Ten Commandments.

Instruction in righteousness is instructions for right living and right living believes in God. One of the foundations of righteousness is found in the life of father Abram. God promised Abram a son; in fact He told Abram the number of his offspring will rival the sum of the stars in the sky and grains of sand. I've been to several beaches and the sand on each individual beach is too many to count – it's a never ending number.

> *Romans 4:13*
> *For the promise that he would be the heir of the world was not to Abraham or to his seed through the law, but through the righteousness of faith.*

We cannot receive the righteousness of God through the law; we can only receive it through faith.

> *Therefore it is of faith that it might be according to grace, so that the promise might be sure to all the seed, not only to those who are of the law, but also to those who are of the faith of Abraham, who is the father of us all as it is written, ("I have made you a father of many nations") in the presence of Him whom he*

believed – God, who gives life to the dead and calls those things which do not exist as though they did;

It was faith according to God's divine influence upon the heart of Abraham that the promise was more than a promise- it was a done deal. Abraham believed and acted on God's promise that he would be the father of many nations and he gave God the glory. Abraham knew God created the heavens and the earth that did not exist until He called them to be. Abraham knew that God called the oceans and the seas to come into existence by the Word of His mouth. Abraham knew God called the dry land out of the sea that did not exist before He called the land to be. Abraham knew God has called life out of the dirt and He knew He called him to be the father of many nations. Faith in God is powerful for anyone who believes.

And not being weak in faith, he did not consider his own body, already dead (since he was about a hundred years old,)" and the deadness of Sarah's womb. He did not waver at the promise of God through unbelief, but was strengthened in faith, giving glory to God, and being fully convinced that what He had promised He was also able to perform. And therefore "It was accounted to him for righteousness

Abraham was around seventy-five years old when God made the promise and he was close to one-hundred years old when he and Sarah became the proud parents of Isaac, a son of promise. Sarah was old and her womb was dead, but God called her womb to life and she produced a son. God acted on the faith of Abraham. He promised Abraham a son and Abraham believed and acted on the promise of God. He was not weak in faith and he did not waver, hesitate, falter, nor shilly-shally. He was fully persuaded, convinced, influenced, and he knew without a doubt that God cannot lie and that God would deliver the promise. Faith in God is better than anything in the world and Abraham's faith in God was accounted to him for righteousness.

12

The doctrine of baptisms

Baptism is a cleansing, purging, or washing through water immersion. It was the ritual for Gentiles to convert to Judaism. It introduced their life in God by symbolically washing away their Gentile ways of life to living a life of His commandments.

John the Baptist's baptism was a baptism of repentance. People came from miles around to hear John preach on the topic of repentance. Repentance is a change of mind about our lifestyle and confessing our sins. The baptism of repentance does not save our souls but is an outward expression of an inward work or change.

The baptism of Jesus and the baptism of the Holy Ghost is one in the same. John specifically said, *"Repent, for the Kingdom of God is at hand,"* in *Matthew 3:2.* Five verses later he says, *"He (Jesus) will baptize you with the Holy Ghost and fire."*

The baptism of the Holy Ghost or the Holy Spirit comes when we truly are remorseful for the life of sin we have been living. We confess these sins and confess we need Jesus as our Savior. The Bible teaches *if we confess with our mouth the Lord Jesus Christ and believe in our heart that God raised Him from the dead, we will be saved. For with the heart one believes unto righteousness, and with the mouth confession is made unto salvation.* When we do this, we are born of God and baptized into the Holy Spirit.

The laying on of hands

The Holy Spirit is also given by the laying on of the hands. An example is in *The Book of Acts 8,* when Philip went to the city of Samaria and preached Christ to the multitude. Unclean spirits were expelled from people who were possessed, the paralyzed and the lamed were healed. When the Apostles in Jerusalem heard about the spiritual move in Samaria, they sent Peter and John to investigate. When they got there, they saw the evidence of salvation and prayed the people would receive the Holy Spirit for they were only baptized in the Name of the Lord Jesus Christ. They prayed and laid hand on them and they received the Holy Spirit. The Teachers and Prophets of Antioch laid hands on Paul and

Barnabas to bless their ministry and confirm their new positions as Apostles, *(Acts 13:1-3)*

The laying on of hands is an act of blessings. When hands were laid on me I was spiritually invigorated, refreshed, and revitalized. It felt like the power of God was roaming through me and I was encouraged. As a pastor I would sometimes line up the entire church in a single file and bless them one by one as I had been blessed. Sometimes the spirit of prophecy would be available and the Lord would share something about the person that only the person knows. This is simply God being God revealing Himself and using His servants to bless others. Other times I would lay hands on people just to encourage them or speak the Word of God over them in prayer.

The laying on the hands is also used for ordination into ministry. It is necessary for the newly ordained person to receive patience, the power, the wisdom, and the love of the Holy Ghost for ministry. It is also used while praying for healing, wisdom, and understanding. When I was a babe in Christ, my brother Vincent from Rhema laid hands on me in prayer for wisdom according to *James 1:5:*

> *If any of you lacks wisdom, let him ask God, who gives to all liberally and without reproach, and it will be given to him.*

After this, I began to have a deeper and truer understanding of my new life. I wanted to learn all I could and my only interest was learning from the Holy Spirit.

As the Spirit wills, the laying on of hands can produce healing for individuals through the spiritual gifts – the gift of healings in particular.

Jesus laid hands on a number of people and healed them: He laid hands on a man that was deaf and dumb and healed him in *Mark 7:31-35*. He laid hands on Peter's mother-in-law in *Matthew 8:2-3* and she was healed, He laid hands on Jairus' daughter and healed her in *Luke 8:54*, He laid hands on a leper and healed him in *Matthew 8:2-3*. Remember, Jesus said greater things we will do as sons and daughters of God because He went to His Father. [See

14

John 14:12] As He healed sick and hurting people through the power of God, so can we.

The resurrection of the dead

1 Thessalonians 4:13-17

But I do not want you to be ignorant, brethren, concerning those who have fallen asleep, lest sorrow as others who have no hope. For if we believe that Jesus died and rose again, even so God will bring with Him those who sleep in Jesus. For this we say to you by the word of the Lord, that we who are alive and remain until the coming of the Lord will by no means precede those who are asleep. For the Lord Himself will descend from heaven with a shout, with the voice of an archangel, and with the trumpet of God. And the dead in Christ will rise first. Then we who are alive and remain shall be caught up together with them in the clouds to meet the Lord in the air. And thus we shall always be with the Lord.

The above Scripture refers to the resurrection of the believers. At the appointed time, at the last trumpet call, all those in Christ will be resurrected from the dead. Every Christian that has lived and died will be brought back to life.

1 Corinthians 15:51

Behold I tell you a mystery: We shall not all sleep, but we shall be changed – in a moment, in the twinkling of an eye, at the last trumpet. For the trumpet will sound, and the dead will be raised incorruptible, and we shall be changed.

God will call the dead in Christ first. It doesn't matter if you were blown up in a million pieces, died in outer space, eaten by wild animals or sea creatures, martyred or died in your sleep, all Christians will be resurrected. Those who are still alive will be caught up (raptured) will meet Jesus in the air.

Jesus describes the day of His coming as a thief in the night. No one knows the time or the date when He will return for His Church.

15

In fact Jesus doesn't know either – only the Father knows. However, we must be ready when He comes.

There's a resurrection of the Body of Christ and there's another resurrection of the dead. Jesus will judge the Church and God will judge the world. The resurrection of the dead refers to all people who were left behind and will be raised from the dead at the end of time for the Great White Throne Judgment.

> *Revelation 20:11-12*
> *Then I saw a great white throne and Him who sat on it, from whom the earth and heaven fled away. And there was found no place for them. And I saw the dead, small and great, standing before God, and the books were opened. And another book was opened, which is the Book of Life. And the dead were judged according to their works, by the things which were written in the books.*

It will be God All-Mighty Who sits on the throne and the heavens and earth will flee from His presence. This group of people will be of every nation, every race, every creed, every dialect, and every color standing in the presence of God.

> *v. 13*
> *The sea gave up the dead who were in it, and Death and Hell delivered up the dead who were in them. And they were judged according to his works.*

It doesn't matter where you died or how you died, everyone will be recalled and judged according to our works. It will be amazing how bodies that have been in decay for thousands of years will suddenly be regenerated. Bodies will change from terrestrial to celestial; or from earthly and native bodies to spiritual bodies. This change will happen in the twinkling of the eye.

Then Death and Hades was cast into the lake of fire. This is the second death. And anyone not found in the Book of Life was cast into the lake of fire. 14 and 15

The eternal judgment of Christ

The way we live will be how we are judged.

John 5:24
Most assuredly, I say to you, he who hears My word and believes in Him who sent Me has everlasting life, and shall not come into judgment, but has passed from death to life.

The system is simple, whoever hears the Words of Jesus and believes that God sent Him already has everlasting life. You will not go to the White Throne Judgment because the White Throne Judgment is for sinners, for those who do not believe in Jesus or that God sent Jesus to earth to offer every man, woman, and child the salvation of the Lord. We have already passed from death to life. This does not mean we will not pass away in our natural bodies, but our spirit man has passed from eternal death and damnation to life eternal with the Lord.

When the Son of Man comes in His glory, and all the Holy angels with Him, He will sit on the throne of His glory. All the nations will be gathered before Him, and He will separate them one from another as a shepherd divides his sheep from the goats. And He will set the sheep on His right hand and the goats on His left.
Then He will say to those on His right, "Come, you blessed of My Father, inherit the kingdom prepared for you from the foundation of the world: for when I was hungry and you gave me food; I was thirsty and you gave Me drink; I was a stranger and You took Me in; I was naked and You clothed Me; I was sick and you visited Me; I was in prison and you came to Me.'
Then the righteous will answer Him saying, Lord, when did we see You hungry and feed You, or thirsty and give You drink? When did we see You a stranger and take You in, or naked and clothe You? Or when did we see You in prison, and come to You? And the King will answer and say to them. "Assuredly,

I say to you, inasmuch as you did it to one of the least of these My brethren, you did it to Me

Then He will also say to those on the left hand, "Depart from Me, you cursed, into the everlasting fire prepared for the devil and his angels: for I was hungry and you gave Me no food; I was thirsty and you gave Me no drink; I was a stranger and you did not take Me in; I was naked and you did not clothed Me; I was sick and in prison and you did not visit to Me.'

Then they will also answer Him, "saying, "Lord, when did we see You hungry or thirsty or a stranger or naked or sick or in prison, and did not minister to You?

Then He will answer them saying, 'Assuredly I say to you inasmuch as you did not do it to one of the least of these, you did not do it to Me,' and these will go away into everlasting punishment, but the righteous into eternal life."

We as individuals will be judged on how we treat people period. If we despise anyone because of the color of their skin, we will not live in the Kingdom of Heaven. If we despise any person for any reason, whether they are short, tall, skinny, fat, dark, light, dialect, intellect, hair texture, social status, or the lack of social status or any other reason, we will be judged and sentenced to the lake of fire and brimstone forever.

He who overcomes shall be clothed in white garments, and I will not blot out his name from the Book of Life.

Defile is to act immorally, to stain your character; it is to live as if you were a heathen. It's a person who says they are Christian but their character does not align with their profession. Those who have not defiled themselves will receive white garments on the Day of Judgment. White garments/linen is the righteous acts of the saints or those who demonstrated godly character while on earth. These white garments are for those who were faithful to God, and exhibited godly character in this life.

18

In *The Revelation of Jesus Christ 3:5*, we find it possible to have our names blotted out, deleted or erased from the Book of Life. This indicates or specifies that a person can become a Christian, claim Jesus Christ as Lord and Savior and have his name written in the Book of Life. However, if this person walks away from the faith, defile his garment, live a corrupt lifestyle, or does not stay faithful to Jesus Christ, his/her name will be blotted out of the Lamb's Book of Life.

> *And the dead were judged according to their works, by the things which were written in the books.*

This verse reveals that someone in Heaven is recording everything we do whether good or bad. This verse should literally scare every person on the face of the earth, especially those who are shaky in their doctrine or lifestyle. But for the saints, the Lamb's Book of Life should be a list of accomplishments, a list of fulfilling Scriptures that pertain to hope and love. It should be a list of caring for one another, giving to one another, exhorting one another, encouraging one another and living according to the will of God working in their lives.

> *Revelation 20:11-15*
> *The sea gave up the dead who were in it, and Death and Hā′dēs delivered up the dead who were in them. And they were judged, each one according to his works. Then Death and Hā′dēs were cast into the lake of fire. This is the second death. And anyone not found written in the Book of Life was cast into the lake of fire.*

The dead will be judged according to their works... If you were a thief, you will be judged according to your works. If you were a liar, you will be judged according to your works. If you were a whoremonger, you will be judged according to your works. If you were a killer, a murderer, you will be judged according to your works. If you were a rapist, sexually immoral or a molester, you will be judged according to your works. If you rejected Christ, you will be judged according to your works. And if you were a leader in the Church and did not preach

19

Christ in truth, and did not operate in the love of Christ, and committed sexual immorality with your members, or stole from them, you will receive a stricter punishment than everyone else. All the big time sinners and all of the dabblers will be judged according to their works.

Jesus told a story how our lifestyle on earth affects our final destination in *Luke 16:19*.

> *There was a certain rich man who was clothed in purple and fine linen and fared sumptuously every day. But there was a certain beggar name Lazarus, full of sores, who laid at his gate desiring to be fed with the crumbs which fell from the rich man's table. Moreover the dogs came and licked his sores.*

There are a lot of people with money who don't have any concern for the poor as the rich man is in this story. This particular man was dressed in the color of royalty, had plenty of wealth, prestige and a host of friends. In terms of prosperity the rich man was the Bill Gates, the Amanain Ortega, the Warren Buffet, the Carlos Slim Helu, or the Michael Bloomberg in that day.

Then there's Lazarus, a beggar who sat at the rich man's gate desiring to eat the crumbs that fell from the rich man's table. However, the rich man passed over him for weeks, months, or even years. He seemed to be in the same condition as the man who asked for alms at the Beautiful gate in *Acts 3*. It is an unfortunate fact there are millions of poor people here in the United States of America –land of the free and home of the brave. There are men and women standing on street corners begging, beseeching, and pleading for money daily– some are legitimate, genuine, and sincere while others use the sympathy of citizens' for financial gain. There are many who make a decent living panhandle all day and then drive home in their Lexus Mercedes or the luxury car of their choice. Because if this, the attitude of many has grown harsh and severe and will not give a dime to any of these people because of the few beggars that are not legitimately poor, and before long hearts are harden because of the actions of a few. This is one of Satan's avenues to trap people into disregarding the poor, ignoring the poor, despising the poor and even hating the poor.

Hebrews 13:2
Do not forget to entertain strangers, for by so doing some have unwittingly entertained angels.

You'll never know exactly who you are encouraging, lending a helping hand, or providing money for a meal. It is true Satan uses kindness for evil and deceit, but the Holy Spirit will lead you who to give to – all you have to do is ask.

So it was that the beggar died, and was carried away by the angels to Abraham's bosom. The rich man also died and was buried. And he being in torment in Hades, he lifted his eyes and saw Abraham afar off and Lazarus in his bosom.

Lazarus died and the Bible says the angels came and carried him to Abraham's bosom. Lazarus went to a place of comfort, a place of peace and rest. He was no longer a beggar trying to eat. The sores on his body had vanished. His tears were wiped away and he was totally healed emotionally, physically, and spiritually. Lazarus is in the place we all want to be.

The rich man also died, he was buried. He didn't go to Abraham's bosom but to hell. Hell is waiting room for evil doers; it is a prelude to the final destination called the lake of fire and brimstone.

In Hades, the former rich man was in horrible torment, anguish, torture, agony, suffering, and pain. He did not display love for anyone but himself and his friends. He had no mercy for those who were hungry and in need. He had no compassion for others outside his friends and family, so his choice of lifestyle sentenced him to eternity first to Hell (A&R) then the Lake that burns with fire (an eternal prison).

Then he cried and said, 'Father Abraham, have mercy on me, and send Lazarus that he may dip the tip of his finger in water and cool my tongue; for I am tormented in this flame.

The rich man was in bad and desperate shape. He was burning in hell, in a constant fire that does not consume the flesh. He looked up and saw Lazarus with father Abraham living in comfort, rest and peace. He called out to Abraham for mercy, something he didn't demonstrate while he was alive, and asked for Lazarus to dip his finger in water and touch his tongue to quench the hurt, anguish and pain he was now experiencing. For years he passed by, stepped over, and treated Lazarus badly, and now he wanted Lazarus to relieve him from his distress.

But Abraham said, 'Son remember that in your lifetime you received your good things and likewise Lazarus evil things; but now he is comforted and you are tormented.

And besides all this, between us and you there is a great gulf fixed, so that those who want to pass from here to you cannot nor can those from there pass to us.

Abraham reminded him of his lifestyle where he lived sumptuously and lavishly, extravagantly and luxuriously in which he laughed and entertained, ate and drank and didn't want for anything. He reminded him of how he treated Lazarus, how he was ignored and frowned upon and neglected and he didn't lift a finger to help him. But the tables have turned and now the rich man wanted Lazarus to dip his finger in water and touch his tongue for relief.

Then he said, 'I beg you therefore, father, that you would send him to my father's house, for I have five brothers that he may testify to them, lest they also come to this place of torment.

They have Moses and the prophets; let them hear them.' And he said, no father Abraham; but if one goes to them from the dead, they will repent."

I believe there are millions of people in this position today. Hell was not made for human beings but for Satan, his angels, his devils, his imps and his demons. Millions of people today are burning in hell because of the choices they made while still living. Rejecting

22

Christ and following the ways of demons and the world will lead you to a horrible afterlife where there is no escape, no parole, no discharge, no commutation, and no mercy. The way you live on earth determines where you live in eternity.

The rich man wanted to save his family from the same judgment and sentence he received by sending Lazarus back to them to warn them on their impending sentence. But Abraham told him they had Moses and the Prophets to show them the way.

Today, we have the teaching of Jesus, the works of Jesus, the love of Jesus, and the sacrifice of Jesus. Today we have the Comforter, which teaches and guides and reveals all the things of God. The problem is a lot of people do not want to hear it; they only want to live their own lives, make their own decisions, they want to be free to do whatever they want to do whenever they want to do it. This life is a temporary life; the real life comes after resurrection.

> But he said to him, "If they do not hear Moses and the prophets, neither will they be persuaded though one rise from the dead.

It is a pity that people sign up for everlasting punishment for a season of fun in the sun.

Fully Equipped

All of these categories play important parts for building ordinary men into extraordinary saints of God. First we must be knowledgeable about who we are in Christ. We must realize the divine influence upon our hearts plays a significant role in the lives of every Christian. When we realize the reality of being One in Christ, One in The Holy Ghost and One with God, then we are able to complete the work of Christ through the Holy Ghost.

There will be times when we will need correction. And there will be times when we correct someone else; we have to do it in love. We should not bash our brothers and sisters over the head when mistakes are made. We should not look down upon them and cast them off. Love plays a mammoth role in our life in Christ. When we are corrected in spiritual matters, we need to receive this correction in love. God chastises, or corrects, or disciplines, or reprimands those He loves. If we receive correction then we will be fine, if we don't, then we are in trouble and will become rebellious against the Lord's instructions.

> *Proverbs 3:5-6*
> *Trust in the Lord with all your heart and lean not to your own understanding; in all your ways acknowledge Him, and He shall direct your paths.*

We should trust in God as Abraham trusted in God. We need to be fully persuaded in Christ, trusting in Him wholly for all things. Also, we should give Him thanks in all things no matter what.

Each and every Christian should embrace the instructions laid out before us in the Bible. We must have an open heart toward the truth of God's Word. There are many things we may not understand but we should never conjure or surmise our own personal interpretation of the word. Personal interpretations are sure fire ways to walk in the darkness.

It is appointed for everyone to die and then comes judgment. The way we live our lives will judge our everlasting home. Our lives should match our belief system in Christ Jesus our Lord, and our works should always be in Christ. Just as Christ only said what the Father says, and did only what the Father does – we should do the same. We must be real in our Christian life. For judgment is coming to the entire world; if you do not want the punishment of the goats, then be obedient to the Word of God as a lamb. Remember, God shears the sheep but He Bar-B-Que's the goats.

God's Sovereignty

Psalms 24:1-2
The earth is the Lord's and the all its fullness, the world and those who dwell therein. For He founded it upon the seas, and established it upon the waters.

God is sovereign. He is supreme; He is the ultimate and absolute God. He created this world and everything in this world and He is the manager of this world. Everything that happens in this world does not slip by Him for He is God. He knows every act of peace and kindness and every act of deceit and violence upon earth. We need to understand this as a Church.

The Bible is the will of God. It is His plan to show His enemies the blessings of those who love Him and the disaster of those who don't. All the events in the Bible have happen, are happening, and going to happen - this is the plan of God. For instance, the Prophets who prophesied about the coming of Jesus were God's plan. When Jesus was born in a manger was also God's plan. When Jesus raised the dead, healed the sick, fed thousands, and taught in parables – this also was the will of God, or the plan of God. His death on the cross was God's plan and when He rose from the dead was also His plan. When Jesus ascended into Heaven and the Holy Spirit came down, this is God's plan for the brothers and sisters in Christ to bear good fruit, to be God's workmanship in Christ Jesus for good works, to be the head and not the tail, above and not beneath, to be strong in the Lord and in the power of His might, to do greater things than Jesus did while He was on the earth as a man. This is all God's plan, and through His sovereignty He will bring His plan to fruition. He will also bring the devil's plan to naught.

Psalms 50:7a-11
I am God, your God. I will not rebuke you for your sacrifices or your burnt offerings, which are continually before Me. I will not take a bull from your house, nor goats out of your folds, for every beast of the forest are Mine, and the cattle on a thousand hills are Mine. I know all the birds of the mountains and the wild beast of the field are Mine.

Christians do not offer God bulls and goats for sacrifices – we never did. The sacrifice of Christians is to present our bodies to God as living sacrifices so His will for our lives will be established and complete. Jesus was the perfect sacrifice and we as the body of

Christ are the hands and the voice of God's will. God is sovereign – He knows all, sees all, and is all powerful.

> *Psalms 50:12-15*
> *If I were hungry, I would not tell you; for the world is Mine and all its fullness. Will I eat the flesh of bulls, or drink the blood of goats? Offer to God thanksgiving, and pay your vows to the Most High. Call upon Me in the day of trouble; I will deliver you, and you shall glorify Me.*

As we matriculate through these last days, we need to keep the truth in the forefront of our minds that all the acts that will be displayed upon the earth will be the will of God. Nothing is going to happen haphazardly, randomly, or arbitrarily.

So when peace is taken away from the earth and men start butchering one another, we need to understand this is the will of God. A lot of people will be killed in a horrible manner and we see these events on the news daily. I don't know how God chooses who will die, and who lives but I will speculate He will use evil people to do the killing for evil is already in their hearts. So I believe He will not use His Church for any evil doing because He is not schizophrenic. So whatever God is doing, the Church needs to be sensitive to His judgments and the role we live as Christians.

Jesus gave a repent or parish teaching one day when people came to him to report that Pilate mingled the blood of some Galileans with their daily sacrifices in *Luke 13*. Jesus asked if the Galileans were worse sinners than everyone else. Then He answered His own question and said, *"No, but unless you repent you will all likewise perish."* We are all going to die unless we are ruptured, the difference is are we living a repented life, are we walking in the newness of life, are we walking in a life where old things have passed away and all things are new, are we utilizing the free gift of the Holy Spirit in our lives according to the will of God. If the answer is yes, then we have passed from death to life, if the answer is no then we will pass from death to eternal death.

Chapter 2

The Light Shineth in Darkness

What is Light

The word "light" is mentioned at least 93 times in the New Testament alone. In the secular world, the word "light" is an event which leads to illumination, spiritual awareness or an act which provides information or clarification. In the spirit realm light is illumination and causes spiritual awareness through an encounter with the True and Living God.

The light is used in similar and different ways in the New Testament. We will examine the Greek definition of five of these terms for light. The first example in Strong's Exhaustive Concordance #1645 – Ĕlaphrŏs, which means 'easy' taken from *Matthew 11:30,* and *2 Cor. 4:17.*

> *Matthew 11:28-30*
> *Come to Me, all you who labor and are heavy laden, and I will give you rest. Take My yoke upon you and learn from Me, for I am gentle and lowly in heart, and you will find rest for your souls. For My yoke is easy and My burden is light.*

This passage of Scriptures has sometimes been referred to as 'The Great Invitation.' In this passage Jesus is revealing Himself as the Giver of life and salvation. It is a call to those who are struggling and bogged down by the cruel circumstances of life in this world. Jesus tells us to come to Him, learn of Him and our lives would be different and far better. There is no pomp in Jesus, no inflated ego, no superciliousness, no superiority complex, and lived

27

without haughtiness. Jesus was the most gentle and kindest and loving person that ever walked the earth even though He was/is the most powerful.

There is no real peace in the kingdom of darkness, only an artificial peace that comes every now and then. It is a peace that never last, the peace of the world is like a fleeting shadow that will change or turn against you at any given moment. But the peace of Jesus, the peace of being born-again is an actual reality that is provided by God the Eternal Father through Jesus the Christ or Jesus the Anointed One.

This is a call to those who have ears to hear and have been trying to obtain eternal life through dead ceremonies, man-made traditions, useless works and fruitless rituals. It is a call for those who have struggled in the darkness and unable to escape no matter how hard they try. This call is for those who are tired of living the way they have been living and ready for a change. These are the people who have heard of God and His great exploits, His wonders and His awesome power, but didn't know Him. They had a mental assent, but nothing more. These are the ones that are hungry for God and are sick and tired of their current lifestyle. However, the people were trapped and yoked to the devil's way of doing things.

Jesus says, "Come to Me," I am the answer to all your problems, all your cares and all your concerns. Join with Me and trust in Me for true rest can only be found in Me. True rest can only come by trusting in Me for who I am and whom I represent.

To be yoked is to be fastened or tied, attached or chained, joined or secured to someone or something. Ranchers make use of yokes for teams of horses. Farmers generally use two oxen with a yoke on their necks so they will go in the same direction. One of the oxen will be stronger than the other so when the stronger oxen turn, the other one turns with it. When we are yoked to Christ, we are tied, fastened, and secured to the King of kings and Lord of lords. When we are yoked, tied or one with Jesus, we are overcomers because Jesus is an overcomer, we can heal the sick because the One we are yoked with heals the sick. We can be holy because the One we are yoked with is Holy, we can be perfect because we are yoked to Jesus.

28

There are many who do not understand our position in Christ or think we cannot accomplish the position Jesus says we can – instead we would rather live under our means and be poor in faith, poor in power and poor in understanding. It's like having a million dollars in the bank but living on 10.00 a week.

When we are One with God, One with Jesus and One with the Holy Spirit according to *John 17*, we are yoked with the Trinity. When we are One in Jesus the Christ, life becomes easier because we are abiding in God the Father, God the Son and God the Holy Spirit and they have come to make their home in us. We don't have to worry about the devil interfering in our lives because the Great Rebuker of Demons dwells in us. We don't have to worry about sinning because we have been born of God. We don't have to worry about our next meal because Jesus is the Supplier of all our needs. We don't have to worry about sickness and diseases because Jesus is The Ultimate Healer – and even if we die due to a sickness or disease, we'll be in the presence of the Lord, which is a healing in itself. The Bible teaches to be absent from the body is to be present with the Lord.

> *John 17:20-23*
> *I do not pray for these alone, (the disciples) but also for those who will believe in Me through their word; that they all may be one, as You Father, are in Me; and I in You; that they also may be one in Us, that the world may believe that You sent Me. And the glory You gave Me I have given them, that they may be one just as We are One. I in them and You in Me that they may be made perfect in one and that the world may know that You have sent Me, and I have loved them as You have loved Me.*

Jesus prayed for the people who would believe His disciple's testimony about Him. When we believed in their word about The Word, we become One with the Father, the Son and the Holy Spirit. Also the world may believe God sent Jesus to this lost and dying world to seek and save those who would call on His Name. The Bible teaches we have received the glory of God from Jesus and we are to give God the glory in all we do.

When we abide in the God the Father, God the Son, and God the Holy Spirit we have the ability to be perfect or different from the world so the world will know that God sent Jesus into this world to change our lives.

Because He physically went to the cross, we will not be punished for our sins because we trust wholly in Him for salvation. This makes our burden light or easy; because the weight of sin would cease to be a burden on us.

> *Matthew 11:30*
> *For My yoke is easy and My burden is light.*

Ĕpiphainō in Strong's Exhaustive Concordance #2014 is defined as: to shine upon, to become visible – *Luke 1:79*

> *Luke 1:79*
> *To give light to those who sit in darkness and the shadow of death, to guide our feet into the way of peace.*

From *Luke 1:67* through *79*, Zacharias prophesied about his son fulfilling the role of Prophet for the Messiah. The above verse declares that Jesus will shine the light of truth to those who sit in darkness. Not only that, but will also be a guide or bring those who are in spiritual bondage into His perfect peace. This is not a temporary peace, but an eternal peace, an ever lasting peace that is beyond our comprehension. This peace is a harmonious and symphonic peace that includes a sweet relationship with the True and Living God.

The spiritual condition of man can be compared to living in darkness all of our life, not able to comprehend, and separated from everything and everyone, but suddenly a light shines on us and around us and causes us to see everything and everyone. We receive spiritual clarity and this changes our lives. An example of this would be the life of Helen Keller. Helen was born blind, deaf and dumb. All her life she could not see or hear or talk. And if she were healed of her infirmities, her life would have changed drastically. She would be able to recognize a cup or a bed, discover the beauty of a lake and the differences in the appearance of people. We receive the same clarity when we come out of the darkness and into the light. I was blind and ignorant but now I see, is the perfect example of this.

Luchnŏs in Strong's Exhaustive Concordance #3088is define as: a portable lamp or other illuminator – a candle or light –Here are two examples in *Matthew 6:22* and *Luke 11:33.*

> *Luke 11:33*
> *No one, when he has lit a lamp, puts it in a secret place or under a basket, but on a lamp stand, that those who come in may see the light.*

Jesus the Christ is the Light of the World and He did not hide the light He was and is. He let every man, woman, and child see the light, or the good that He is. He did this so every person could see there is a better way to live, a godly way to live. So we as the body of Christ should not hide the light of Christ that dwells within us. The purpose of the body of Christ is to be a reflection of the light of Christ, to let the light of Christ manifest in us, to be shown to all who are in darkness so they may have the same chance to escape the wiles of darkness as we did.

> *Luke 11:34*
> *The lamp of the body is the eye. Therefore, when your eye is good, your whole body also is full of light. But when your eye is bad, your body also is full of darkness.*

It has been said, "You are what you eat." But even more so, you are what watch and see. That's why David proclaimed he would not set anything before his eyes that is evil. [See *Psalms 101:3*]

In this day and time, we see evil actions every day. We see evil or the results of malevolent deeds on the news, we see immoral activities in movies and television shows. We see wickedness on the

31

highways and streets in our cities, states, country and the world. We see evil in our grocery stores, laundry mats, parks, in our homes and neighborhoods. So it is almost impossible to go to a place where evil is not present. However, God did not leave us hopeless; we won't be swayed by evil because the Holy Spirit that abides in us. Our job is not to be influenced by what we see but by the Word of God. *Greater is He that is in us then he that is in the world. 1 John 4:4.*

We have to work to take care of our families, and our jobs often include people who are not saved, or people of the world. People are not hired because of their spiritual position; they are hired for their experience and skills to get the job done. Christians often find themselves like a fly in a gallon of buttermilk, surrounded by the people of the world. Our ears are assaulted everyday by the conversation of the world. Our eyes are attacked daily witnessing the lives of those who do not know God or even respect Him as God. However, when we abide in God we can live in this cruel and evil world and not be affected by it. We are in the world and not of the world.

John the Baptist was surrounded by heathen men and women but he did not focus on the ills of the world but told them to repent and be baptized. Jesus sat with sinners, whores, tax collectors and hypocrites, but that did not sway His walk with God. Paul dealt with a multitude of personalities as he traveled the known world preaching the Gospel, but his mind stayed on the prize of the high calling of God. The same Holy Ghost that abode in Jesus, John, Paul, Peter, James, and the rest of the heroes of the faith, now abides in us, if we are born-again.

Remember bad company corrupts good morals and many people have been taken down the wrong road because they did not guard themselves against worldly vices. The things they saw, heard, and felt had power and dominion over them instead of having dominion and power over the things they saw, heard and felt. I have found that the best way to handle this is to line it up with Scripture, is this an evil act, or a Godly act? If it is an evil act then we should act according to what the Bible says about the situation. If it is a Godly act, we should smile because you witnessed another brother or sister in the Lord working in the will of God.

What a lamp is to a room, the eye is to the body. The lamp only has one purpose, to give light in the room. "When your eye is good…" or "single" in the King James Version, you will have only one goal in mind, one purpose or one pursuit and that is total devotion to God. When a person is single minded, his mind is not divided between God's way of doing things and the world's way of doing things, but it is stayed on the course that was given. Single mindedness will keep brothers and sisters in Christ from being double minded and thus unstable in all our ways. Single mindedness is achieved by abiding in the Word and the Word abiding in you. Single mindedness is achieved by living by the Word of God because the Word of God is living in you.

If we do not see Jesus as God's total package for salvation, Jesus the Light of the world, then our eye is bad and spiritual darkness will have place in our lives.

Luke 11:35
Therefore take heed that the light which is in you is not darkness.

This speaks mostly of deception. We must make sure that the light in you is not an artificial light, or darkness imitating light. An artificial light is not a pure light, or a true light. It is not a light at all, it is a fabrication of light and is a tainted, deceptive image of light, and is designed to plant doubt and unbelief in God's Word – this false light is active, especially when it comes to the doctrine of Christ Jesus our Lord. Remember that Satan appears as an angel of light to deceive people. So an artificial light is a false light and a false light is not of God but of the evil one. There is nothing false in God and Christ.

So we must be careful of what we hear and how we hear. We must live transparent lives and examine ourselves daily so we don't deceive ourselves or let others deceive us. To take heed is to watch out, be aware, and be cautious and alert. The devil is like a roaring lion roaming the earth seeing who he may devour through deceit and evil suggestions. We must make sure that the light in us is a pure and clean light so that others will know there is a God in Heaven.

Luke 11:36
If then your whole body is full of light, having no part dark,
the whole body will be full of light, as when the bright shining
on a lamp gives you light.

This is the problem with the some of the churches today; it is part dark and part light. It is people that make up the Church and it is the Church's responsibility, business, and obligation to tend to the spiritual needs of the people and physical needs when warranted. Jesus told Peter to "Feed My sheep." In order to feed the sheep, each and every member must be, should be born-again and operating in the ways of the Lord. This is the reason God gave gifts to the Church so that it would be healthy and thriving. So when we are sold out to Christ, walking in His ways, loving our brothers and sisters and worshipping God; the whole body will be full of light, as when the brightness of a lamp gives you light.

Phōs in Strong's Exhaustive Concordance #5457 is defined: to shine or to make manifest – fire or light – lustrous, i.e. well-illuminated, bright full of light – *Matt. 5:14.*

Matthew 5:14
You are the light of the world. A city that is set on a hill
cannot be hidden.

Jesus told His disciples, and other men and women who would be born-again;we are the light of the world. Christians should be full of light; we should be vibrant and alive, vivacious and energetic in Christ Jesus. You should be recognized as a Christian by strangers because you are a light as Jesus is the light.

John 1:1-4
In the beginning was the Word, and the Word was with
God, and the Word was God. He was in the beginning with

34

God. All things were made through Him, and without Him nothing was made that was made. In Him was life, and the life was the light of men.

Jesus is the epitome of light. He is the personification, the embodiment, the essence, and the quintessence of Light. He is the Originator, the Creator, Instigator, the Designer, and the Initiator of Light and of all that follows. Jesus is the light and when we are born-again, we become light as Jesus is light. We, those who are born-again, are the light of the world. As the world watched Jesus, they should also take note of His Church. When we are the light, we are love. When we are the light, we are peace. When we are the light, we are a reflection of Christ and proof that God sent Him to the earth to redeem us from ourselves and the devil. Remember, we are One in Christ as Christ is One in us. We are One with God and God is One with us, according to the Scriptures in *John 17*. Since we are Christians (Christ-like) then we should be the light of the world. We are assigned from God above to be a witness to those who are in darkness. Jesus is the Light of men.

The Church, the collection of born-again believers, are supposed to be a reflection of the light of Christ. Every person in Christ should be as transparent as possible in order to let the pure light of the love of God be seen by all of those who are in darkness. We should not hide the light of Christ in our lives but should let His light illuminate, make manifest and lustrous for all to see because the Gospel is for everyone.

In the following verse we find two lights in the same sentence but different meanings. In *Matthew 5:15* it says

> *You are the light of the world. A city that is set on a hill cannot be hidden. Nor do they light a lamp and put it under a basket, but on a lamp stand, and it gives light to all who are in the house.*

In Strong's Exhaustive concordance #2545, the first light in the verse is from the Greek word, "Kaiō" and it is defined as to set on fire, or to consume – to burn. Therefore, the first part of the verse

35

would say that no one sets a lamp on fire to hide the light.

The second light is also a Greek word, this one is lampō, it is a Greek verb, which means to radiate, or brilliancy – to give light. This light in Strong's Exhaustive concordance #2989, it means to radiate, to glow, to illuminate, to light up, and to shine or gleam.

So this verse can be understood as; No one sets a candle on fire and sets it under a basket where it doesn't do anyone any good, but it is put on a stand, or propped up to radiate the entire room. The light of Jesus is the truth that radiates through the world to exhibit the truth of God. To bring knowledge to those who were once darkened or obfuscated.

Let your light so shine before men, that they may see your good works and glorify your Father in heaven

Jesus did not do His work in secret and we also should not do the work of the Lord in secret. Jesus stood before the multitudes and healed the sick, cleansed the lepers, cast out demons, raised the dead, fed multitudes, and corrected those who were wrong in their doctrine and wrong in their lifestyle. He did not pull any punches nor did He compromise His mission in bringing the truth to those who hated Him. And in everything He did, He glorified God the Father.

Since Jesus is the true light, and we are abiding in His Word and His Word is abiding in us, we should be the reflection of the light of Christ; since we are vessels for holy use; since we are being molded into His image, and since we are sons of God and have surrendered our lives so He may work through us as He did in Christ Jesus, we have to listen and follow the instructions of being light bearers.

Chapter 3

He Loves This!

What God Loves

John 3:16-17

God so loved the world that He gave His only begotten Son, that whoever believes in Him should not perish but have everlasting life. For God did not send His Son into the world to condemn the world, but that the world through Him might be saved.

John 3:16 is probably one of the most famous Bible verses in the world. We see people at sporting events holding signs advertising *John 3:16*. There are bill boards by highways proclaiming John 3:16 and there are panhandlers on corners with cardboard signs declaring the same. My friend David Hinton sings about 'The night Jack Daniels met *John 3:16*,' how it changed his life.

God loves this world because He made this world. He knew from the beginning that Adam would sin, but He loves us anyway. Some take this as a license to sin, but God's grace is not a license to sin. God gives the entire planet an opportunity to make plans for life eternal. This physical life is just the test run; our real life is with Christ in Eternity. So God sent Jesus to introduce to the world the True and Living God. That's love. God gives us numerous chances to choose Christ and change our lives. Jesus lived as a man, but He taught as God about what was expected of us and how to gain everlasting life. God so loves us that He sent Jesus to die on the cross (the form of capital punishment of the day) for the sins of mankind, for the mistakes we have made, for bad judgment and the crimes we've committed on others. Now God loves Jesus, He also loves mankind and He has given us the opportunity to get in His plan by choosing Jesus over all the other gods that has the world in its sway.

Jesus did not come to condemn the world (society) He came to set us free from ourselves and the wiles of the devil

God loves a cheerful giver

2 Corinthians 9:7
So let each one give as he purposes in his heart, not grudgingly or of necessity; for God loves a cheerful giver.

God loves people who are cheerful givers. He loves those who give because it brings them joy to give when others are in need. God gives to us and we should give to each other. When we are happy about giving, we should realize it is one of the signs of your salvation. When we were lost, about the only time we gave was to get something in return. And there are philanthropists who give to various institutions and causes without knowing God. Yes, they are doing a good deed but it is in vain if you do not know Jesus. We cannot give our way to Heaven, it is only through Christ. So the gifts of philanthropists are temporary, but in Christ giving is eternal.

If you don't want to give, you might as well keep it in your pocket. God doesn't want you to give grudgingly, or reluctantly, or stingily, or even resentfully. For if you have these characteristics in your heart, and then you might as well keep your money, and buy yourself a steak dinner somewhere. However, when you don't give, no one will give to you in your time of need.

Acts 20:35
"It is more blessed to give than to receive."

We, as Christians must support the weak for everyone is not strong in the Lord and in the power of His might. Everyone is not a Spiritual giant. Everyone is not a mature Christian. In fact I believe there are a lot of babes in Christ in every church.

Our laboring is not for riches, it is for the lost souls to receive

38

salvation, and taught the ways of Christ. Although money is needed for the spread of the Gospel, it is not our primary purpose. For the clergy, you are blessed when you give the true Word of Christ Jesus our Lord.

When Christianity was known as the way, the Church was going about the Father's business. They were praying in one mind and one accord, meaning all minds were on Christ and the mission that was given to the Church. At one point, everyone that was able sold all their possessions and laid them at the Apostle's feet and no person lacked anything. We are truly blessed when we all are on the same page – praising our Savior, following our Savior, and being blessed by our Savior.

Freely you have received – freely give.

God loves faithfulness.

God's definition of faithfulness is holding on and believing in Him no matter what the circumstances may look like or what you may feel like. As a pit-bull clamps down on a pork chop and doesn't let go, we should clamp down in our walk in Christ and don't falter. As we all know, looks can be deceiving. You may be in a situation that may look very scary, very bad, and disastrous. It may look as if there is no way out of the situation and your back is against the wall. What would you do? Would you run around to try to find someone to help you avoid the cataclysm you seem to be destined for? Would you remember that God is your source and that He has promised to look out for you?

In *The Gospel of Mark*, there is a story of a little girl who was dying. As Jesus went to heal the little girl, another woman with an issue of blood, or some type of bleeding disorder, had distracted Him momentarily by touching the hem of His robe and He felt power leave His body.

She didn't bother to ask for a healing; her faith was so strong she knew she would be healed if she could get close enough to touch the hem of His robe.

As He was telling this faithful woman, *"Your faith has made you whole,"* a religious leader came to the parent of the little girl and said, *"The girl is dead, don't bother the teacher any longer."* The religious leader believed the situation had gone too far and nothing or nobody could help the girl because she was dead. He had no faith in the Lord Jesus Christ. He had put the power of God in a box and ultimately denied the fact that God couldn't do anything about the situation. He failed to realize that God can do anything except fail.

I want to point out something that is very interesting; the religious leader had probably witnessed the interlude between Jesus and the bleeding woman. He was right there with the parents of the little girl and all who were close both saw and heard the exchange of Jesus and the woman with the issue of blood. He had to be there when the woman explained how she had spent all of her money with all of the doctors and still could not get healed of this disease. But yet and still, he told the parents, *"Don't bother the teacher anymore. The girl is dead."*

Jesus didn't pay any attention to the unbelieving leaders, but said to the parents, *"Do not be afraid only believe."*

When He got to the house, there were people at the house crying and wailing on the loss of the little girl. With all the people grieving and weeping and wailing, it would be easy for a person to say, it's too late. The majority has spoken and they are acting on what they believe. It is a good thing that God doesn't take a vote that allow the majority to rule or make decisions.

But Jesus again, refused the bad report, and retold the parents, "Do not be afraid, only believe." So He was standing on His faith in that the healing, or the raising of the dead, would be accomplished in the power of God according to the Scriptures. It didn't matter what anyone thought or what anyone said – Jesus knew the little girl will receive her life. As Jesus watched the people carrying on, He said, *"Why make this commotion and weep? The child is not dead, but sleeping."* But the people didn't believe Him and ridiculed Him. In other words, they called Him crazy, a fanatic, or even demon possessed, and said He didn't know what was going on. But Jesus ignored them. He didn't plug in to their system of doubt and unbelief. If He had taken heed to the obstacles, the girl would remain dead. Jesus had to ignore the screaming of the world's unbelief because it was contradictory to His Gospel.

So He simply put them out of the house because their unbelief would be a hindrance to the recovery of the little girl. He put them out because they were not worthy to witness the power of God in raising the girl from the dead. You must be wary of unbelieving believers in your camp. It could crush or quench the move of the Spirit if you are not careful. Faith comes by hearing and so does unbelief.

In *Luke 4:18*, He told the people in the synagogue He was here to preach the Gospel, heal people, mend the broken hearted, proclaim liberty to the captives, to free those who are oppressed, raise the dead and cast out demons. This was the Word of God, so if Jesus paid attention to the people, and took heed to their unbelief, He would have fallen short of His purpose on the earth. He had to remain faithful to what God had called Him to do. Yes Jesus was called by God to do these things in order to reconcile man back to God. And the little girl was a step in completing this purpose.

God loves faithfulness. Jesus was faithful and God rewarded Him with the healing of the young girl. Let us look at this a little closer.

Jesus set out to heal the little girl; however she died along the way. That can devastate a person. But Jesus took no note of that. In fact He was adamant in standing on the Word that He had spoken earlier. He had to refuse to give in or concede to the death of the girl. His faith was faithful.

In our lives today, we have the Word of God. In life, there are circumstances that would try and make you disunite from your faith in the Word of God. There may be some qualifying factors that look real enough, and feel real enough to shake you from your faith in God's Word. When you focus on these qualifying factors, then you are not focused on the Word. The people were looking at the controlling factors in the little girl's condition, but Jesus was looking at the power of God. These two will always be opposite of one another.

Jesus had to ignore the negative thinking and speaking of the people that were around Him. Today, there are a lot of people who have taken it upon themselves to say that God doesn't heal anymore, or God doesn't deliver anyone anymore, God is not in the miracle business anymore. They are constantly saying that God doesn't to this or God doesn't do that. The only reason they say these things is because the devil has filled them with doubt and unbelief. Like the religious leaders, they chose what is safe to believe so they would not be associated with their own failure. But God says He is *the same yesterday, today, and forever.* What He did in the Old Testament, He will do in the New. What He did for David, Esther, Moses, Ruth, and Joseph, He will do for Mark, Sally, Garold, Bob, Robert, Gary, John and Shaniece. Faithfulness requires believing, and faithfulness pleases God. To the people, it was a miracle, but to Jesus – it is a way of life.

Because of steadfast faithfulness, God rewarded Jesus and the family of the little girl with complete restoration by raising her from the dead. It was faithfulness that brought this about. God rewards those who are faithful to His Word with restoration, deliverance, and complete wholeness. The Bible says the eyes of God are searching the world over trying to find the Word being spoken so the Word will complete the task that it was set out to do. [See *2 Chronicles 16:9*] Faithfulness in the Word will work wonders in your life.

When the nation of Israel was backed up against the Red Sea and Pharaoh's army was in hot pursuit. They didn't have anywhere to go. The army was on one side and the sea on the other. Most of the people didn't understand what was going on so they talked only of what they knew. They only knew of what they had been accustomed to for the past four hundred plus years. They didn't know this was the opportunity to let God be God and to show the world there is only one True and Living God.

To be fair, the only relationship Israel had with God at that time was a one of prayer for release from the Egyptians. They knew He was the God of their forefathers and He is the Supreme God of the Universe but that information did set in. Their relationship at that time was a distant one. They only knew a little about Him, because He hadn't fully revealed Himself to them. After God unveiled Himself to them through Moses as I AM, the True and Living God, they were expected to be faithful to Him. His love for them was His act of revealing Himself to them as their God while at the same time, revealing Himself as an enemy to those who worship false gods as the Egyptians did.

Another example is found in *The Book of Acts.* From chapters

2-8 we see the growth of the Church. We see that God added to the Church daily and great miracles were performed through the Apostles. Then as usual, some haters of the Gospel tried to find a way to make one stumble. The enemy chose one of the first deacons named Stephen, a man full of the Holy Ghost and wisdom. They tried to trick him as they did with Jesus and they came with the false accusations as they did with Jesus. In fact, the accusations of Jesus and Stephen are almost identical. [Compare *Luke 23:2* and *Mark 14:56 – 59* with *Acts 6:11-14*]

Stephen was stoned to death and again, like Jesus, he forgave them as they were killing him. The religious leaders liked this so much; they began persecuting all who believed in Jesus as the Son of God. A young man named Saul got letters from the High Priest to put Christians in jail and possibly kill them for their faith.

Now with the naked eye, this incident seems terrible – persecuting the Church. But the disciples were to go and preach the Gospel; instead they were still in Jerusalem. So God used this incident to scatter the saints so the Gospel would be preached as Jesus commanded them to do. For instance, Philip went to Samaria and preached Christ there. The result was that *many people who were paralyzed and lame were healed, and unclean spirits came out of many that were possessed. And there was great joy in that city.*

> Acts 1:8
> *"But you shall receive power when the Holy Spirit has come upon you; and you shall be witnesses to Me in Jerusalem, and in all Judea and Samaria, and to the end of the earth."*

If the Apostles did not get persecuted, they would have stayed in Jerusalem. But the persecution served to further the Gospel of Jesus Christ. So things may have looked bad but as the epistle says, all things work for the good for those who love Christ.

There are some churches that do in house evangelism. In fact, they will witness to their brothers in Christ and fellowship with the world. Most of the churches are stuck with their week-to-week routines. Go to church on Sunday and go to work throughout the week, party on Friday night, the game, shopping and tea parties on Saturday and back at church on Sunday morning.

But when a crisis hit, the person's heart will turn in search for someone who's associated with God. The reason for God's persecution was to spread the Gospel because people have a tendency to get lazy and just rest. Comfort has an inclination to lie down and call themselves blessed and not spread the Word as God has commanded to do.

So when we find ourselves in persecution, we might want to check ourselves – Are we doing what God has called us to do or are we just being lazy? Remember all things work for the good for those who love Christ Jesus our Lord. So we must be faithful to the Word, to the mission, and to the Lord of Host.

Conditions

It is unfortunate that a lot of times, the Word of God is not practiced in the context in which He meant it to be practiced. For instance, when we read the promises in the Bible, we find there are conditions to these promises. There are many who desire the end result without meeting the conditions. Here are a few examples:

Acts 16:31
Believe on the Lord Jesus Christ, and you will be saved, you and your household.

Romans 10:9
That if you confess with your mouth the Lord Jesus and believe in your heart that God raised Him from the dead, you will be saved.

In Acts the condition is to believe on the Lord Jesus Christ. The result is that *you and your household shall be saved.* In Romans the condition is to confess the Lord Jesus and believe in your heart. If we confess Jesus but don't believe in our heart, then we have not met the condition necessary for salvation. If you do not believe God raised Him from the dead, then you have not met the condition for salvation. We must be believers!

James 4:8
Draw near to God and He will draw near to you.

First we have to draw near to God and then He will draw near to you. The condition is to draw near to God; the result is that He will draw near to you.

James 4:10
Humble yourselves in the sight of the Lord, and He will lift
you up.

Again, the condition is for us to must humble ourselves in the sight of the Lord, then He will lift you up is the result. We must pay attention to the entire verse in the Bible. We must meet the conditions God has set for us to live a spiritually productive life.

An example of this is going to the store to buy a can of green beans. You go to the store and pick the can of green beans you desire, go to the checkout lady but you do not have the money to purchase the item. The condition is that you pay for the item; the result will be ownership of the item. If you don't pay for the item you won't legally own the item; if you do not confess the Lord Jesus and believe in your heart that God raise Him from the dead, you won't have salvation.

Notes:

Chapter 4

He Hates That?

What God Hates

God has to be amused with our conversations and our actions. Our opinions about Him have been so diverse that one would wonder if they were talking about the same God. In most cases they're not. The opinion about God generally runs from one extreme to another. Some people have God painted as an all knowing entity who sits on the throne of Heaven with a big stick ready to swat us at every wrong we do. On the other hand, some people believe they can do whatever they want to do and have the blessing of God rest on their lives.

In this chapter, we will look at what God says He hates. We will attempt to straighten out most of the misconceptions of what people in general think and say about Him. We will also look into His Word to see what He says about the things that displease Him.

We are called to serve Him, we are to serve our brothers and sisters in Christ, we are to fulfill His purpose upon this earth, and also in our lives. So in order to be productive in the Kingdom of God, we need to know what God loves and what God hates. Remember these are not my ideas of what His Word means. We must understand that God says what He means and means what He says.

In *Proverbs 6:16-19* we get a list of what God hates. The first six are the things He hates, and the seventh is an abomination to Him:

> *These six things the Lord hates, yes, seven are an abomination to Him:*

An abomination is described as something that is extremely dis-

47

liked and abhorrence to Him. Abhorrence is something loathsome and disgusting. So when God calls something an abomination He is saying He has an extreme hatred for it. He has an extreme distaste, detestation, an absolute disgust and loathing. Abomination fills Him with repugnance and a deep seeded loathing. Needless to say that God is not happy with abominations.

Here are some examples of abominations are found in Strong's Exhaustive Concordance: In Hebrew # 8441 – the word is described as something disgusting.

> *Leviticus 18:22*
> *"You shall not lie with a male as with a woman. It is an abomination".*

God created man and woman to worship Him, have dominion over the earth including all the animals that crawl, walk, slither, fly and swim. We were created to take care of each other, to love each other, to help each other, produce children and teach them the ways of God. This is God's intent for every person born of woman, for without a woman, we cannot be born into this world.

The original intent for man and woman is to be fruitful and multiply. God's intent was to fill the earth with man and beast in harmony and in agreement. We are to live congruently in the freedom in which God created for us to walk in. But God's good and holy intentions were twisted by Satan's influence with natural and carnal man and the act of homosexuality was born. We do not know where it first started, but we do know that God destroyed two cities because the men in these cities practiced this abomination openly without any refrain. The men of Sodom and Gomorrah also wanted to have sex with the angels of the Lord. In God's anger, discuss, fury and wrath, He destroyed both cities by raining fire and brimstone upon them.

Sex between a man and a woman is an awesome thing and produces an aura of love in the purest form. Sex between a man and a man can only produce the stench of feces and lubricants. It is not a natural act and it something that God loathes.

48

8251 – Filthy, especially idolatrous as found in *Zech. 9:7*

> *I will take away the blood from his mouth, and the abominations from between his teeth. But he who remains, even he shall be for our God. And shall be like a leader in Judah.*

The blood from his mouth and the abominations between his teeth refers to the close of unlawful and idolatrous practices. Blood is a sacred thing, it the life that flows through our veins; to be without blood is to be without life. Demonic entities tries to encourage unlawful sacrifices through shedding innocent blood to appease gods and drinking blood in honor of these demons posing as gods.

God said, *"You shall not eat the blood of any flesh, for the life of all flesh is its blood."*

When I read this verse I think about all the vampire movies, and zombie movies that act as if they are drinking human blood or eating human brains. Of course these movies are fiction and meant for entertainment but there are people who are swayed by them to the point they become obsessed with the drinking of blood. Also, there are serial killers who drink the blood of their victims. Sometimes, life and fiction are so emerged; it is hard to the difference. But God says blood is sacred, and it is an abomination for those who consume it.

946 – Detestation, abhorrence dislike or hatred as in dilatory. Dilatory is being slow, or lazy, or negligent, or slack.

> *Revelation 17:5*
> *"And on her forehead a name was written: Mystery, Babylon the Great, The Mother of Harlots and of the abominations of the Earth."*

This verse refers to the harlot church that will arise in the last days. In fact there are many harlot churches today that rejects God and His Christ. But in the latter days, a church will rise above the nations and will be full of abdominal acts

These are just a few examples of abominations. There are more, but for the purpose of this subject, we will stick to a few that are more prevalent.

The first set of things that God hates in this passage is:

v 17
A proud look, a lying tongue, and hands that shed innocent blood...

Strong's Exhaustive Concordance #7311 tells us the word 'proud' means to be high, to exalt oneself and to be haughty.'

A proud look in this passage is talking about the attitude of self-worth and a superior attitude over everyone else. It is what we call today, a superiority complex. It is a defiant attitude of one who looks down on people and believes they are of less value. Most of the time, we can find this type of behavior in the upper classes of society. Some of these people have the tendency of looking down on lower classes with disdain. These folks are commonly called nose snobbers.

Another close related type of pride is found in sports figures. These are those who have been blessed with tremendous physical ability. They can do things that other sports figures cannot do. They have excelled in their profession and are at the top of their game. After a period of time of indulging in fan worship, it generally goes to their heads. Some sport figures often find themselves in jail or prison because pride has puffed them up to believe that they are above the law, and they can do anything they want. They talk about how good they are and a lot of times they will prove to everyone they are just that good.

Lucifer had this same characteristic before he fell from the grace of God. This self-exaltation is a prelude to trouble in one's life. It starts with thinking of yourself more highly than you ought to think. After a period time in thoughts of invincibility, indestructability, in-vulnerability, and insuperability, you will begin to put your thoughts into actions. And through your actions, you will find yourself in trouble both spiritually and physically.

It is not just sports figures that become prideful, there are also television personalities, business men, models, movie actors and actresses, and musicians who acquire the same complex after they have made so much money or have won so many awards. We see this attitude every day. There are businessmen and women who have become great in what they do. But they become proud and defiant and a lot of times they believe they are above the law, even the law of God.

This is also true in some government positions. The thrill of power corrupts and absolute power corrupts absolutely or completely. The pride syndrome has overpowered many kings, presidents, dictators, prime ministers and so on through the history of time. Many rulers who have tasted power have been some of the most sinister leaders in the history of man. Pride has given men a strong desire to rule the world. Why? Carnal men like Satan, want to be worshipped. They want to be called great and be admired; they want all those who are not like them to worship them.

The one thing that is constant about pride in self is that it is followed by a fall. We see this in the lives of all the Pharaohs, Hitler, Napoleon, Alexander the Great, and all the Caesars, just to name a few. They wanted absolute power and to be worshipped as an absolute deity. But each one who had these prideful desires fell to their deaths.

Proverbs 16:18
Pride goes before destruction and a haughty spirit before a fall.

A haughty spirit is a spirit that is arrogant. Arrogance is a synonym of pride or an overbearing pride. So arrogance and pride are twins, and they go together hand in hand. They are so tightly wound together; you will hardly find one without the other.

God hates a Lying Tongue

Another characteristic of what God hates is a lying tongue. A lie is portraying something false as true. It is a false statement, or series of false statements that are deliberately presented as being the truth. It is an action deliberately portrayed to deceive or to give a wrong impression.

In the early days of the Body of Christ or Church, men and

51

women were selling their properties such as land and houses and laid the proceeds at the feet of the Apostles. The Church witnessed the philanthropic gift of a man named Joses who sold his land and brought the money and laid it at the Apostle's feet. People were impressed; they were so impressed that a man and his wife Ananias and Sapphira sold a possession in order to be as popular or noble as Joses. However, Ananias only gave a portion of the sale to the Apostles while claiming that he gave it all.

> *Acts 5:3-11*
> *But Peter said, "Ananias, why has Satan filled your heart to lie to the Holy Spirit and keep back part of the price of the land for yourself? While it remained, was it not your own? And after it was sold, was it not in your own control? Why have you conceived this thing in your heart? You have not lied to men but to God."*
> *When Ananias heard the words of Peter, he fell dead. The young men arose and wrapped him, carried him out, and buried him. About three hours later, Sapphira came in but she did not know what happened to her husband. And Peter addressed her,*
> *"Tell me whether you sold the land for so much?" She said "Yes, for so much." Then Peter said to her, "How is it that you have agreed together 'to test the Holy Spirit of the Lord?' Then he said, look the feet of those who buried your husband are at the door, and they will carry you out also. Then immediately, she fell down at his feet and breathed her last. And the young men came in and found her dead, and carried her out and buried her by her husband. So great fear came upon all the church and upon all who heard these things.*

God hates lies! This couple thought they could impress their neighborhood with their giving but their actions were deceitful. Peter said, "why has Satan filled your heart?" Satan is the author of everything bad. Here, he wooed Ananias and Sapphira with a deceitful sense of popularity, admiration, and fame as humble philanthropist, and they paid for it with their lives.

Revelation 21:8
But the cowardly, unbelieving, abominable, murderers, sex-
ually immoral, sorcerers, idolaters, and all liars shall have their
part in the lake which burns with fire and brimstone, which is
the second death.

Some people say there are white lies and black lies. God didn't say He hated black lies and loved white lies or vice versa. He says that He hates a lying tongue. Anything that is presented as true, but is not – He hates.

In the entertainment world, there are movies, especially religious movies, which portray Christianity in a false light. Something as serious as Christianity should always be portrayed as God intended it to be portrayed. But there are movies that cast doubt on the deity of God and His Christ. There are movies that portray priest in a web of light that is not holy in character and they treat the temple of God as a profane thing. The problem with this is that it causes people who do not know the Word, to believe the lie the movie portrays. These movies are fiction, a fable, a fantasy and fabrications portraying a lying truth – or selling lies as the truth as a form of entertainment.

Matthew 18:6
But whoever causes one of these little ones who believe in
Me to sin, it would be better for him if a millstone were hung
around his neck, and he were drowned in the depth of the sea.

Jesus talks about deception. When a person deceives a little one, or children of God with falsehoods about His Deity, about our salvation, about our character and conduct – the Bible says that whosoever deceives a little child is in big trouble and it would have been better if the deceiver had never been born.

Because of movies, there are several million people who believe that devils can't walk on church grounds. They believe that Jesus didn't really die on the cross for our sins. They believe that Jesus wasn't raised from the dead. They believe there will be a second war in Heaven. They believe Satan will come when his thousand years of imprisonment is over in order to have sex with a certain woman so their offspring can overthrow God.

Hollywood writes these stories as fiction; however, seeds are planted into the minds of the simple. When the simple waters these seeds with more movies they become more disillusioned with the truth. Disillusionment will lead to ignorance, ignorance will lead to confusion and confusion will lead to darkness and darkness will lead to death. It is a domino effect.

Cable stations also contribute to the madness with their programs like the Da Vinci Code and other programs that contradict the Word of God. Since faith comes by hearing, then doubt and unbelief will come by hearing also. These are lying tongues and God hates a lying tongue even if it's for entertainment, it brainwashes some folks subtly.

Hands that Shed Innocent Blood

There is a special breed of people in the world that kill others for fun, for money, for power, for prestige, or for no reason at all. Throughout history, there have marauders, bandits, plunderers, looters, and pillagers who go to and fro looking for victims. Taking a life doesn't mean anything to them; it is as meaningless as a discarded pop can. In today's society, a person can be shot and killed just walking down the street, or having a burger in a fast food restaurant, or at the movie theater, or at a shopping mall, or even in their own house. God hates the act of shedding innocent blood.

This brings us to the subject of abortions. Surely fetuses will fall into the category of innocence that is uncorrupted by wickedness even though it was conceived in the flesh. Fetuses do not get the chance to do anything good or evil. Since God hates the shedding of innocent blood, then abortion would be something that God hates.

The judicial court system has killed many people who were thought to be guilty of the crime of murder, only to find out later they were innocent. Many people have lied in open court, sending innocent men and women to their deaths that are sanctioned, authorized, indorsed, and approved by the State. To God, there is no difference between a liar and a murderer. But He hates those who rush to shed innocent blood. And there are many innocent people who have died due to outlaw justice by hanging, crucifixion, beheading, burning at the stake, or firing squads. Some were just at the wrong place at the wrong time.

Jesus was as innocent as they come, He committed no sin in His entire life yet false witnesses were hired to shed innocent blood. The same happened to Stephen, one of the first deacons who was stoned to death because he was true to the Word of God.

A Heart That Devises Wicked Plans
Proverbs 1:8-19

"My sons, if sinners entice you, do not consent. If they say, "Come with us, let us lie in wait to shed blood; let us lurk secretly for the innocent without cause; let us swallow them alive like Sheol, and whole like those who go down to the pit; We shall find all kinds of precious possessions, we shall fill our houses with spoil; cast in your lot among us, let us all have a purse."

My son, do not walk in the way with them, keep your foot from their path; for their feet run to evil, and they make haste to shed blood.

Surely in vain the net is spread in the sight of any bird; but they lie in wait for their own blood. They lurk secretly for their own lives. So are the ways of everyone who is greedy for gain; it takes away the life of its owners.

This particular passage speaks of shedding innocent blood and planning to do evil. This segment in Psalms talks about three of the categories of activities that God hates which is listed in *Proverbs 6:* Planning evil, planning to shed innocent blood, and feet being swift to run to evil. Those who plan evil will find that evil has its own plans for those who participate. These people will find themselves caught in the same trap they have set for others. Much like the verse above, hands that shed innocent blood, *Proverbs 1:18-19* sheds a little light on the two things that God hates.

Planning evil is planning an action that is against God's will, His purpose, His laws, and against the doctrine of Light. It is causing harm to others, such as stealing from others, robbing others, lying on others, killing others, raping others, worshipping other gods, sacrificing children to false gods or committing your kids to prostitution. Planning evil is to practice these shady arts of the kingdom of darkness for material gain, financial gain, or sport. To plan evil is to premeditate, plot, design, and organize, to form a strategy with the purpose to harm another human being, physically, emotionally or spiritually.

Have you ever noticed how people are caught in committing crimes? When a person sins, or commits crimes against people, or property, they will eventually get caught. The prisons are full of people who got caught. Many have plotted and schemed and contemplated how to commit a crime without getting caught. Most are not successful. The Bible says that snares are visible; traps are seen, and even though they see the trap, they are still snared by the trap. There aren't any successful bank robbers, drug dealers, murderers, white color embezzlers, thieves, pimps, and con artist that live the life of luxury for very long. What you sow will be what you reap. Whether it is going to prison, going to the graveyard, or watching your body whittle away with disease and viruses, there is no such thing as a perfect crime – even if it takes years to be discovered, it will be discovered. And on Judgment Day these activities will be judged.

A False Witness Speaking Lies

Jesus was a victim of false testimonies and lies when the Jewish council charged him:

Mark 14:56-58
For many bore false witness against Him, but their testimonies did not agree. Then some bore false witness against Him saying, "We heard Him say, 'I will destroy this temple made with hands, and within three days I will build another made without hands."

At the trial just before the crucifixion of Jesus, these men were grasping at straws, so to speak, to bring incriminating evidence against the Son of Man. They reached into their limited minds and quoted, very badly I might add, words that would send Jesus to His death. These were false witnesses and even though they were misquoting Christ, the intention in their heart was on doing evil. They wanted to kill the Savior of the world.

A false witness lives and thinks in a cloud of darkness. False witnesses are liars. And liars who deceive are themselves deceived. Like the people in Psalms One, these people will fall into their own traps.

Throughout the ages false witnesses have put many to prison, death and the grave. False witnesses have testified in court fabricating events that weren't true. Some are false witnesses to obtain money, some are false witnesses to acquire property, some are false witnesses to stay out of jail, and some are false witnesses to climb the corporate ladder. In the Scripture above the false witnesses were trying to fabricate a testimony that would send Jesus to the cross. The Pharisees wanted to get rid of Him and they hired men to give false testimony to end the Jesus problem. They used these false witnesses to kill their competition because many believed in Jesus as the Christ.

This is something that a false witness and a liar choose for himself. First he must deny the truth, when a person denies the truth; he opens the door for deception to come into his life. He can no longer discern the difference between what is true and what is false. The lie has become a part of him; it becomes something as natural as brushing your teeth.

One Who Sows Discord Among the Brethren

One of the worst things that can happen in any church is a brother or sister who sows discord in the body. If I've seen this once, I've seen it fifty times. People, even some church people have gotten bent out of shape over the silliest things. A brother may not like the style of worship or the preacher or teacher. So he or she would pull another member of the body and talk about how much they don't like this or how much they don't like that. This should be done this way or that way, or if I were doing it I would do it like this or like that.

When a person talks against one of the brothers in Christ, it is called sowing discord and God hates this. The Church/Body of Christ is supposed to operate in one mind and one accord. This means the Church should be going in the same direction and everyone in that particular body of Christ should be in agreement. The words the people should be speaking should be words of edification. We are not called to tear down one another; we are called to build one another up. If a person is sowing discord, he is doing the devil's work in creating disunity in the body of Christ.

Many times, the person who sows discord in the Church is often a young person in the Lord, or they are unschooled in the ways of the Lord. He may have grown up in church physically, but he is stale spiritually. Understanding is just beyond his grasp and most often these people are looking at the physical realm for answers instead of the spiritual realm.

For instance, I have seen some people get upset because there was too much praise and worship in a service and they just wanted to hear the word spoken. I have seen people get upset because there was too much word and not enough praise and worship. I have seen people get upset because there were ushers at the door. I have heard people complain because the praise music had a country flare to it, or and R & B touch, or a pop music style or the old negro spiritual style of music that is different from what they are accustomed to.

Whatever the situation, people do not like something different. So they will talk about it with someone else. You will hear, "well, I don't believe the way they do." Or "That is not of the Lord." "Those guys this or those guys that." You should know that they are sowing discord and we need to disassociate with them.

Discord tears relationships and churches apart. Disunity causes division, hurt feelings and even violence. I've even seen a brother hit another brother in the head because he felt the brother had too much authority. So if you are speaking against members of your church, stop it and begin to speak life into them. Come in agreement with God and speak the same thing that God speaks. God hates those who sow discord among the Church.

Proverbs 6:12-15
A worthless person, a wicked man, walks with a perverse mouth; He winks with his eyes, he shuffles his feet, He points with his fingers; Perversity is in his heart, He devises evil continually, he sows discord. Therefore his calamity shall come suddenly; suddenly he shall be broken without remedy.

God calls a man that has uses corrupt communication worthless. The characteristics are a man that winks with his eye and is animated with his body limbs. This man lives this type of lifestyle naturally and is good in the art of deception or in today's vernacular, a con man. A heart of perversity is an evil heart and his only goal in life is causing disruption, strife, and trouble in general. This man may have run games on folks for a long time but he will eventually experience catastrophe, without a remedy. Remedy here is translated as a cure. So there will not be any help for the person that lives this lifestyle.

This seventh thing is also an abomination unto the Lord. As we have discussed earlier, an abomination is something that the Lord God has an extreme dislike to.

Malachi 2:11
– Judah has dealt treacherously. And an abomination has been committed in Israel and in Jerusalem. For Judah has profaned the Lord's Holy institution, which He loves: He married the daughter of a foreign god.

In the natural, the covenant relationship of marriage is highly esteemed by the Spirit of God. He instructs believers to seek a believing partner to insure holiness in marriage. The word bond means they are fasten together, or tied together. When a man and woman marry, they become tied and fasten together when their marriage is consummated. The two become one. So when a Christian marries a person that is an unbeliever, then he/she has polluted the body with a foreign substance. The body or the marriage is not holy because you have joined with an unbeliever or a harlot. You cannot mix God with the Devil; you cannot mix the Holy with the unholy. The foreign substance here is a different belief system, a different god, or a non-Christian way of life.

He also requires just and faithful attitudes because unfaithfulness will destroy this sacred covenant and produce divorce. We must obey God and marry in the Lord and be loving and faithful to your marriage partner. When problems do come we must reject divorce as an answer to martial problems. So by all means, a couple should do all they can to keep the marriage intact. In order to do this, one must be willing to relearn love, and if necessary relearn understanding and forgiveness.

In the spiritual realm, we have become one with the Lord Jesus Christ. This means that our bodies do not belong to us anymore; we have become one with the Father and the Son and the Holy Spirit. When we worship any other god than our heavenly Father, we are committing spiritual adultery. This means we are not being loyal to the True and Living God. God says that we have become whores when we go after other gods. This includes people going after other religions that do not accept Jesus Christ as the Son of God. Whores are not respected in the physical realm and certainly not in the spiritual realm.

The first commandment tells us that we should serve no other god. God is a jealous God and He calls this an abomination when one of His children goes after other gods. In *The Book of Judges*, we have seen God allow heathen countries to come and chastise His children who have gone after other gods.

Today, the question at hand concerns Jesus. There are so many religions in the world today that it would make your head spin. Some are called religions and some are called ways of life. But they people fail to understand there is no life without Jesus Christ. If Christ is not in it, then we as Christians should not be in it.

When a person adopts a religion that is not Christ centered, then

God calls it an abomination. It is something that God Himself, extremely dislikes. These are His Words, not mine. When we accept a way of life that is not based on the principles of Christ, then God is not pleased. When we go to someone other than God or those who are ordained by God, He is still not pleased.

If there is one thing we must understand, is that there is only one way to Heaven and that is through Christ Jesus. There is only one correct way to live and that is lined out in the New Testament. The Epistles especially show us the right way to live. If we line our lives the way God has planned for us, then we will be pleasing and victorious in everything that we do.

> *Proverbs 8:13*
> *The fear of the Lord is to hate evil; Pride and arrogance and the evil way.*

Since we are called to be the dwelling house of the Lord, we should line ourselves up with God's opinion and His ways. If He hates something, then we should hate the same thing that God hates. If we love something that God hates, then we are outside the will of God. We wouldn't be of the same opinion as God. And we will not be useful in the Kingdom of God. God hates evil, He hates pride and He hates arrogance. Since He hates it, we should hate it also.

> *Proverbs 11:1*
> *Dishonest scales are an abomination to the Lord, but a just weight is His delight.*

Cheating people is an abomination unto God. We are to be honest in all of our dealings with one another. We should not short-change anyone. We should not run up the prices during a time of crises, and we should not take advantage of the poor.

During the recent hurricane, people were jacking up prices to make a bigger profit. God calls this taking, 'advantage of people.' God did not call us to beat people out of their money by extortion and price gouging (swindling). He called us to be givers even in difficult times.

Proverbs 11:20
Those who are of a perverse heart are an abomination to
the Lord, but the blameless in their ways are His delight.

To have a perverse heart is a terrible thing. Perverse is directed away from what is right and good. To be perverse is to be awkward, headstrong, stubborn, and tenacious. To be perverted is to be depraved, corrupt, degenerate, and a deviant. They are both the opposite of what is right and good. It is corruption.

There are people who dream about being perverted and these characteristics start from the heart. There are people who dream about rapping children, molesting the elderly and even farm animals. Doctors call these traits diseases, but God calls it sin, an abomination, something that He detest and calls it repulsive. The only way to treat a perverse heart is to be born-again.

Proverbs 15:8-9
The sacrifice of the wicked is an abomination to the Lord,
but the prayer of the upright is His delight. The way of the
wicked is an abomination to the Lord; But He loves him who
follows righteousness.

The sacrifice of the wicked today would be to go to church with something other than pleasing the Lord, or seeking the Lord, or doing service in the Lord on your mind. The children of Israel were sacrificing animals to the Lord but their hearts were far from the Lord. They were just going through the motions to get it over with so that they can go and 'be themselves.'

The sacrifices of people today are showing up to church with their minds on something else. Their bodies are in church, but their minds are on the football games, or basketball games, or waxing their car, the woman or man they met last night, paying bills, getting their hair done, thinking on circumstances at work, or a thousand other things of that nature. They don't want to be there but they are making a showing and all the while, most are hoping that services will end soon so that they can go back to their heart's desires.

Sacrificing is also giving money without being grudging, unwillingly, stingily, or reluctantly. It should be a joy to give, to share, and provide for others that cannot provide for themselves. However, for most people on the planet, the idea of giving to the Lord is as far away from their minds as the east is to the west.

If a person calls himself doing something for the Lord but His heart is not in it; then the sacrifice is worthless and you have wasted your time. God is looking for pure hearts that want to serve Him because they love Him.

Another part of a sacrificial abomination are those who go to church just for show, or to check out the ladies, or the men, or to hustle the church out of some money, this is also an abomination unto the Lord. Some folks figure they could spend some time in church to be seen and labeled as a church-goer for future references, and respected as a prominent person. God says even the prayers of these people are an abomination to the Him. Why? It is extremely hated by God because these prayers are selfish and self-seeking. The prayers are generally geared not to help someone in need; they are to satisfy their own greed.

If a person is practicing righteousness, then you are a delight to the Lord. When you are doing the Father's commands, you would be the reason for the smile on God's face. *Proverbs 37:4* says to *delight ourselves in the Lord and He will give you the desires of your hearts.* It is a good thing to be a delight in the Lord and to walk in the gift of His righteousness.

Prayer

May the God of our Lord and Savior Jesus Christ, the Father of glory, give to me the spirit of wisdom and revelation in the knowledge of Him. I pray that the eyes of my understanding are enlightened so that I may know the hope of His calling in my life.

Reveal to me Father to know what is the hope of Your inheritance in the saints, Your church and the exceeding greatness of Your power in me because I believe, according to the working of Your mighty power which You worked in Christ when You raised Him from the dead and seated Him at Your right hand in the heavenly places, far above all principality and power and might and dominion, and every name that is named, not only in this age but also in that which is to come.

In Jesus Name, AMEN.

Notes:

Chapter 5

A Man Sent from God

John the Baptist

God always informs man when a change is coming. He doesn't have to, but He does. Throughout the years of mankind, God spoke to His kings, Prophets and Priest to announce His intentions. One of the many examples can be found in Isaiah:

Isaiah 9:2
The people who walked in darkness have seen a great light; those who dwelt in the land of shadow of death, upon them a light has shined.

The Scripture-prophesy tells us that people were walking in darkness, walking around in confusion, sin and death; but now they see a great light. Upon the planet earth, folks that were living in the land of the shadow of death have seen a light. They saw the absence of chaos, confusion, error, ignorance, disobedience, willful blindness and rebellion in this wonderful light. They saw peace in the light and everything that is good. The Word, which is Jesus, spoke to the Prophets and told them what was about to happen in order to prepare the people of the earth of the forth coming changes.

For instance, in *Genesis 15* He told Abraham his descendants would be enslaved for 400 years; and they were. Another example of this is found in `*Genesis 18:17* when God said, *"Shall I hide from Abraham what I am doing?"* In this example, God informed Abraham that He was about to destroy the people in the land of Sodom and Gomorrah because their lifestyle was corrupt. Just as any loving

65

Dad informs his children, God informs us of things to come. He has done it over and over again throughout history.

God the Son spoke to Isaiah around the eighth century BC. The Light, (Jesus), was coming for those who have been enslaved by darkness. There was hope on the horizon. There was anticipation for the ones who were looking to the hills from which their help was coming. Isaiah prophesied by the Word of the Lord about the Light that would shine upon the lost people on the earth. The divine knowledge of the universe was coming to give mankind a choice between serving the darkness and death, or serving the Light and life.

Approximately 740 years later, God ordained another Prophet to proclaim the coming of the Light that exposes the darkness and the sins of the world.

John 1:6
There was a man sent from God, whose name was John. This man came for a witness, to bear witness of the Light, which all through him might believe.

Notice it reads, *"A man sent from God,"* John did not just show up, for he was sent by God for a specific purpose. John the Baptist was born – to bear witness of the Light coming into the world. In other words, it was John's job, or purpose in life, to introduce Jesus as the Son of God, as the Light of the World. He was to testify of the true Light which the Prophets had previously testified about a few thousand years earlier. God is so sovereign; He called John the Baptist before the foundation of the world to introduce the Spirit of Truth to the spirit of error. John's calling was to present The One who would expose the dark hearts that was in every man, and to show those who are ignorantly disobedient the way of repentance. To open the eyes and give insight to those who were willfully blind. John was born to introduce the Light to start the process of reconciling men to God.

The Kingdom of God is at hand was his message. Repent from your sins and be baptized for the remission of sins, was his instructions.

John stayed true to the message God had given him, even unto death.

The birth of John the Baptist is a parallel with the birth of the Patriarch Isaac, the son of Abraham. Like Abraham, John's father, Zacharias, was an old man with a barren wife. Both Isaac and John were miracle births from old women. However, John's purpose in life was different than that of Isaac. Isaac's purpose was to be a patriarch of the Nation of Israel; John's purpose was to introduce the world to Christ.

John had an effect on people before he was even born. Mary, the mother of Jesus came to visit Elizabeth in the hill country one day and when Mary entered the house and greeted her cousin, John leaped in his mother's womb and she was filled with the Holy Spirit. So John and Jesus are the few people in the world born filled with the Holy Spirit.

Luke 1:80
So the child grew and became strong in spirit, and was in the deserts till the day of his manifestation to Israel.

John was Spirit-filled before he was born but I want you to notice he still had to become strong in the Spirit. Becoming strong in the Spirit requires spending time, or communing, with the Lord. John spent time with God and was trained by the Holy Spirit, as is the custom for serving God. John was in training in the ways of the Lord until the day of His manifestation to Israel. In other words, he was in training until he graduated and the grace (the ability) of God was clearly seen in him as he preached repentance and baptized all who would hear.

It takes time to grow in the Spirit of God. We grow in the Spirit by reading the Scriptures, prayer, and praise and worship to our Lord. We grow in the Spirit by listening to what The Holy Ghost has to say about any subject – and all the subjects of life are found in the Bible. We grow in the Spirit by being obedient to what the Bible teaches and God has a way to confirm what you have read. When we take that first step, God rewards us with understanding. The more we dive into His Word, the more revelation knowledge He gives us. God rewards those who diligently seek Him.

Matthew 7:7-8

Ask, and it will be given to you; seek and you shall find; knock and it will be opened to you. For everyone who asks receives, and he who seeks finds, and to him who knocks it will be opened.

I was baptized at the age of ten. I grew up in church but I was only a friend to the Church because I did not apply myself to learn of Him. I had read parts of the Bible but I didn't understand what I was reading. I knew the stories of Adam and Eve, Noah and the ark, David and Goliath, Sampson and Delilah, and the feeding of the five-thousand. But I only had head knowledge of these events. It wasn't until I really got serious and repented of everything I could think of earnestly and set my face toward God to my life changed. The awesome power of God came over me and it was so strong, that nothing else mattered. The world of evil was lifted from my shoulders and I had a peace that I did not know or understand. But I sure welcomed it. I went to my room and spoke in a language that I had no knowledge of for three days straight and then several times during the day. I found out later that it was the gift of tongues and I was edifying myself or stirring up the Spirit of God within me. For the next three years I would spend ten to twelve hours in my prayer language and study before the Lord put me to work teaching His Word. But the most amazing part was I understood what the Holy Spirit was telling me. My life was forever changed.

John the Baptist spent many years in the wilderness with the Spirit of the Lord. His diet was locust and wild honey and again the Bible tells us that he was filled with the Holy Spirit from the womb, (See *Luke 1:15*). Neither wine nor strong drink ever touched his lips. He grew up in a place that did not have very many distractions other than nature. There weren't any television shows or movies; there weren't any sporting events, or corporate expansions, shopping for food or paying bills, or any other activities that plague the human race today. He didn't have the time for wine; women or song, the only thing he was interested in was the activities in Kingdom of God.

With all distractions aside, the Lord spent quality time with John the Baptist and trained him in His ways to prepare him for ministry.

It is a fact that men and women who are called to the ministry should be trained by the Holy Spirit. There are many men and women that love the Lord and accept Him as Savoir but not Lord in their lives. Most people do not want to go through the yielding, the learning and the partaking of Him that is necessary to be powerful in God as they are meant to be. Moses was in the backside of the dessert for forty years before he went to Egypt. Jesus spent thirty years on the earth before He started His three and a half years of ministry. Paul spent three years in the dessert and another fourteen years in Arabia before he went to see the disciples. So Paul spent a lot of time in quietude before he started teaching and preaching the Gospel. We should learn this lesson from these men of renown and spend quality time with the Lord so we can truly know Him, His voice, and His ways before we can truly minister to others. We may not have the chance to spend 30 or 40 years in quiet solitude with Him, but we can certainly make time for God on a regular basis. We simply cannot minister to the children of God without knowing the ways of God.

Luke 4b-6
The voice of one crying in the wilderness: Prepare the way of the Lord; Make His paths straight. Every valley shall be filled and every mountain and hill brought low; the crooked places shall be made straight and the rough ways smooth; and all flesh shall see the salvation of God.

Many people recognized John as a Prophet who speaks the Word of God. He did not hold back any punches. When he saw many of the Pharisees and Sadducees coming to his baptism, he said to them, "Brood of Vipers! Who warned you to flee from the wrath to come? Therefore bear fruits worthy of repentance, and do not think to say to yourselves, 'We have Abraham as our father.' For I say to you that God is able to raise up children to Abraham from these stones.

John did not mix his words nor did he hold back what needed

to be said. John called the religious leaders sons of snakes. There is
no doubt the light of John's preaching was calling them to examine
their selves. He told them they needed to do the right thing in their
lives by bearing fruit worthy of a changed life for the glory of God.
Don't rely on Abraham as your father; rely on God because He can
make sons of Abraham out of rocks.

John wore camel's hair with a leather belt so he was a sight to see.
But even so, a lot people from Jerusalem, Judea, and the entire region around the Jordan went to him and were baptized in the Jordan
and confessing their sins. John was fulfilling the Scriptures by preparing the way of the Lord. He was making the crooked places or
paths straight. His preaching and baptizing was making the rough
ways smooth as he set up his cousin Jesus as the Lamb of God.

v 8
He was not that Light, but was sent to bear witness of that
Light.

John was only the forerunner to the light. He was God's witness
of Jesus, the Light of the World. The Jews sent priests and Levites
from Jerusalem to ask John if he was the Christ. Of course John
answered "no" and the committee questioned Him further asking if
he was Elijah or the Prophet to come? Again he said no. It is interesting to note that John did not realize that he was operating in the
spirit and power of Elijah. His focus was on the Kingdom at hand.

The committee just couldn't leave it at that, they persisted in
their line of questioning because their mentors/superiors were waiting for answers to this strange phenomenon that was happening in
their midst. It was John's ministry they did not authorize and the
leaders wanted some answers.

When John the Baptist started quoting Isaiah, *"I am the voice of
one crying in the wilderness; make straight the way of the Lord."* It confused the students and they missed the point of what John was saying.
They should have been familiar with that passage of Scripture about
the coming Messiah but they didn't see it. They did not recognize the

passage from Isaiah, but they should have because these students by Jewish law started reading and memorizing the Torah and the Scriptures at the age of five years old. They asked, *"Then why are you baptizing if you are not the Christ, or the Prophet or Elijah?"*

Again, John the Baptist testifies about Christ while he reveals his own position, *"I baptize with water, but there stands One among you whom you do don't know. It is He who comes after me, is preferred before me, whose sandal strap I am not worthy to loose."* In other words, John was saying. "Hey, I'm just the point man. I am nothing compared to the One that's coming after me. He is so great, so holy, so all of that, that I am not worthy to untie His shoes. My job is simply to warn you that a change is coming according to the Word and ways of God."

The power of John was not one of working miracles such as healing the sick and raising the dead. His power was in his declaration. He was a herald proclaiming the change coming to the earth. His purpose was to announce to the world that the Kingdom of God was at hand. He was announcing the death sentence for the kingdom of darkness and to introduce the Light, the way to salvation for all that wanted to escape from their dark and treacherous ways of life.

John the Baptist was the early edition, or breaking news to introduce the plan of God and to prepare His people, informing them to repent from the works of the darkness. For the Light was coming to expose the works of the darkness and to offer an opportunity to walk in the light. Jesus said *there is none greater than John the Baptist.*

He was not that Light, but was sent to bear witness of that Light. That was the true Light which gives light to every man coming into the world.

John the Baptist was not the Light; he was preparing the way for the Light. His message to the people was to repent. To repent means to change your way of thinking, this will in turn change your way of living.

An example of his ministry was to tell the truth about the judgment that was coming to the earth. He told King Herod he was in violation for marrying his brother's wife. Not only was Herodias his

71

brother's wife, but also his niece. John pulled no punches, he declared right to be right and wrong to be wrong. God was bringing change to the land of Israel and subsequently, to the world. John the Baptist was the instrument that God used to introduce His Son into the world

v 9
That was the true Light which gives light to every man coming into the world.

John 1:29-31
Finally the day came when John saw Jesus coming and he proclaimed, declared, and decreed, to the crowd, "Behold! The Lamb of God, who takes away the sins of the world. This is He of whom I said, 'after me comes a Man who is preferred before me, for He was before me.' I did not know Him; but that He should be revealed to Israel, therefore I came baptizing with water"

John was excited! The years of preparation had come to fruition because the Son of God was walking toward him. *Behold the Lamb of God Who takes away the sins of the world!* John finally got the chance to introduce Jesus to the world. The people around him finally got a glimpse of the One Who would save them from their sins. The people did not truly understand what was going on but they watched as John the Baptist and Jesus the Christ came together.

Matthew 3:13-14
Then Jesus came from Nazareth to John at the Jordan to be baptized by him. And John tried to prevent Him saying, "I need to be baptized by You, and are You coming to me?

John knew Jesus was the Son of God. He knew Jesus was greater than he was. Remember he said 'I am not worthy to lose His sandals.' Yet here he was watching the Christ come to him wanting to be baptized by him. John was taken aback. This should be the other way around. I believe his mind was running a hundred miles an hour.

This is the Son of God – the Creator of the earth and everything in it, on it, above it and below it.   The Lamb of God who would bare our grief's and carries our sorrows. The One we esteemed stricken, smitten by God, and afflicted. This is the One that would be wounded for our transgressions and bruised for our iniquities. This is the One that the chastisement for our peace would be upon and by His strips we will be healed. It should be Jesus that baptizes me.

> *Matthew 3:15*
> *But Jesus answered and said to him, "Permit it to be so now, for thus it is fitting for us to fulfill righteousness." And then he allowed Him.*

Jesus was not a sinner so He was not baptized for committing any sin. Jesus was baptized in order to join with the other Israelites that were baptized by John to confirm the ministry of John. The Father wanted Him to be baptized by John the Baptist to fulfill righteousness.

> *When He had been baptized, Jesus came up immediately from the water; and behold, the heavens were opened to Him, and He saw the Spirit of God descending like a dove and alighting upon Him.*

The kingdom of darkness trembled when it witnessed Jesus coming up out of the water and the heavens opening up so the Spirit of God would descend like a dove and rest upon the One that would put an end to their reign of terror on the earth. At that time, Satan knew the eternal time clock began counting down to his demise, and he became desperate because Salvation was about to snatch men out of his grasp of doom and gloom and into the arms of the Lord.

The Relationship – God the Father and God the Son

God and Jesus have the most excellent relationship ever! God and Jesus are the epitome of one mind and one accord. They are One! They are in tune with each other. No fractions, no divisions, and no disunions, but are in perfect unity. To be in one accord is to be on the same page, have identical thoughts, and have identical character and attributes. They have the same qualities and aspects. Jesus and God are One! They were in agreement when God sent Him on a mission to earth to seek and save that which is lost. This was God's plan all along, before the beginning of time. Jesus would be the answer to the troubles of man in the earth. Adam was flesh and bone when he signed the earth's least over to Satan. So Jesus had to redeem the least Adam lost as flesh and bone,(as Adam was). Even though Jesus was sent by God, He had to live as a human being. He had the emotions of a human being, He ate like a human being, drank like a human being, and He even required sleep as a human being, but He was also a vessel of the power of God on earth. He set the example of how all Christians should be.

God's plan was for Jesus to complete His plan. The duty of Jesus as flesh and bone was to allow the Father to work through Him to accomplish the task of salvation for mankind - *Luke 19:10*, to do God's will - *John 6:38*, bring in everlasting righteousness - *Daniel 9:24*, destroy the works of the devil - *Heb. 2:14* and *1 John 3:8*, fulfill the Old Testament - *Matt. 5:17* give life - *John 10:10* and *28*, abolish ceremonialism - *Dan. 9:27*, and complete revelation - *Heb. 1:1*.

John 5:19b
Most assuredly, I say to you, the Son can do nothing of Himself, but what He sees the Father do; for whatever He does, the Son also does in like manner.

Jesus is setting the example for us, as the Father did – Jesus did. As born-again sons of God, we must embrace what Jesus taught by example. So the example is what God loves, we should love. What God hates, we should hate. What God does, we should do.

It is not so much as the miracles that He did, it is the compassion He had for everyone, and it is the love that produced action in meeting the needs of the people. Because God so loved the world He sent Jesus to show the love of God in His walk, in His talk, and in

His ways. Jesus was emulating God while He was on the earth. And in this, He glorified God.

For as the Father loves the Son, and shows Him all things that He Himself does; and He will show greater works than these that you may marvel. For as the Father raises the dead and gives life to them, even so the Son gives life to whom He will.

There are a lot of people who say they know Jesus. But the most important thing is - does Jesus know you? Have you made the effort to get into the Bible and learn of Him? Have you spent time in the Spirit, in His presence – soaking up the awesome atmosphere of His existence, and His Company? Do you separate yourself from everyone to be still before the presence of God? This is how Jesus and God related to one another and as the Father showed the Son all things, God will show us all things. Jesus demonstrated the need to help others in whatever condition they are in, so they also may have life in Christ Jesus.

For the Father judges no one, but has committed all judgment to the Son, that all should honor the Son just as they honor the Father. He who does not honor the Son does not honor the Father who sent Him.

What are you going to do with Jesus? As I have said several times throughout this book – If you do not accept Jesus, you do not have God. It will be Jesus who will make the final judgment on your eternal address according to your faith in Him, (or lack of). Let me tell you a secret, you will judge yourself by your actions, your conversations, your belief system, and your love. Jesus will just confirm your actions and pass on your sentence.

John 5:24
Most assuredly, I say to you, "he who hears My word and believes in Him who sent Me has everlasting life, and shall not come to judgement, but has passed from death to everlasting life.

75

When we get real about Jesus and believe in Him we will not go to the heavenly district court to be judged, but we have passed from death to everlasting life. Notice the tense "has passed". This is not an event that is going to happen, it has already happened. It happened the moment you believed in Jesus as the Christ. Before we came to Christ, we were living in death and hell was our reward. But when we received spiritual clarity in Jesus the Messiah, Jesus the Christ, we passed from death to life.

You search the Scriptures, for in them you think you have eternal life; and these are they which testify of Me. But you are not willing to come to ME that you may have life.

There are many, many people who scan the Scriptures, glance over the Scriptures, or take a peek or two at the Scriptures and come up with an omelet recipe, or a live free/care free lifestyle. When we search the Scriptures our hearts need to be open to receive understanding. When we rightly divide the Word of truth in humility with strong desire to learn of Him, God will open the eyes of your heart and allow His revelation to be manifested in your spirit. I remember when I read parts of the Bible and was deflated because I was not born-again, born of God and therefore could not understand the things of God. I read that Israel was the chosen people and I did not qualify because I am not an Israeli. We perish for lack of knowledge.

I do not receive honor from men. But I know you, that you do not have the love of God in you. I have come in My Father's name, and you do not receive Me, if another comes in his own name, him you will receive.

Isn't it funny that some did not and do not believe in Him. After all the miracles, the walking on the water, the feeding of thousands with a two piece fish dinner, raising the dead, healing the sick, giving sight to the blind, cleansing the lepers, and demonstrating dominion over nature refused to believe He is, was, and forever will be the Son of God. However, if an ordinary person delivers a great motivational speech, the people would pawn over him/her as if they were deity. There are thousands of Christians following men instead of God. There are thousands of 'Christians' who call on the Name of Jesus and don't know Christ. There are thousands of Christians who follow Pastors and Prophets, Bishops and Apostles who don't read their Bibles. We as the race of human beings have the tendency to believe what we see with our eyes and don't believe what we don't see. We walk by sight and not by faith when the Bible declares *"We walk by faith and not by sight."*

It is interesting that Jesus did not get the respect as the Prophets of old. If Ahab (as evil as he was) respected Elijah as a Prophet of God, why couldn't the Pharisees, Sadducees, and Scribes recognize Jesus as the Son of God. The reason is because the sects of that day believed they had already arrived in spiritual maturity and were comfortable in their way of life. Jesus said He *did not come to call the righteous, but the sinners to repentance. Luke 5:32.*

> *How can you believe, who receive honor from one another, and do not seek the honor that comes from the only God?*

Jesus says we need to stop slapping our brothers and sisters on the back and honor God. There is nothing wrong with encouraging one another, helping one another, lifting up one another; but the bottom line is God deserves the glory for all we do. He deserves the glory in our praise, He deserves the glory in our worship, He deserves the glory in our evangelizing, preaching and teaching, and He deserves the glory in our lifestyle. Let us not make our Pastors, Teachers, Bishops, and Evangelists 'gods' because they are serving God also, but let us seek the true glory that comes from the true and living God and not from each other. The ultimate glory we can give God is sincere work in His Kingdom. The ultimate glory that comes from God is *"Well done, My good and faithful servant."*

Jesus and God communicated daily. Jesus knew the voice of His Father because He had a relationship with His Father. *I and My Father are One. John 10:30.* Since they are One, they remain in full contact with one another. Furthermore, the Bible teaches that we, the body of Christ, are also one with Jesus, one with God the Father and one with the Holy Spirit. We, the Church of God, the children of God, the Body of Christ and as the family of God also have the privilege of hearing from God through the Holy Spirit, and the ability to be receptive to the voice of the Lord, because He declared that we, born-again believers, are one in the Trinity.

As Jesus heard from God, then we the Body of Christ also have the privileged to hear from God though the Holy Spirit. Jesus says, *"My children" hear my voice and the voice of another, we will not follow.* This is because we have a relationship with God, Jesus, and the Holy Spirit.

The Devil will try to talk you also, pretending to be God. Remember, he comes as an angel of light to steal, kill, and destroy. He will attempt to take you in a different direction, (to the Lake if Fire). So if you are not sure if you are hearing from God, make sure the voice that is talking to you lines up with the Bible. If what is said is in the Bible, and in the context of which it was written, then you are hearing from God or a messenger of God. If what is said does not line up with the Word of God then it is the enemy of the Trinity trying to get your attention and get you extradited from the Kingdom of God.

Notes:

Chapter 6

Jesus Christ - The Anointed One

Jesus

Every person on the planet should love Jesus for what He has done in our lives. The job and task He did for mankind is a job or task that only one person could do; and that was Jesus the Christ, or Jesus the Anointed One. Even though He is All-powerful, All-knowing, Ever-present and Eternal, He was still the most humble man that ever walked the face of the earth. Even though He was the Son of God, sent in human form, He was still obedient to the will of the Father to save mankind from the clutches of evil. Even though He was tempted with all the temptations that has plagued mankind, He lived without committing one sin. He lived and felt the pain, the agony, the sting, the anguish and the suffering of mankind so He knows what we are going through. He was obedient to do the Father's will, to save sinners, to bring everlasting righteousness, to fulfill the Old Testament, fulfill the Law, to abolish ceremonialism, to complete revelation and *to destroy the works of the devil.* There is no other man, group of men or legions of angels that could have accomplished what Jesus accomplished for you and me.

His character was perfect for He was and is still holy, still powerful, still righteous, still just, still guiltless, still sinless, still spotless, still innocent, still meek, still merciful, still humble and still forgiving all day, every day. With all the mess that man had gotten into, it took a man that fit all these characteristics to bring man out of the darkness and into the light.

Jesus the Christ – The Anointed One wore many hats and He is recognized by many different people for the many different acts, miracles, phenomena, and wonders which changed the lives of men for the better and still changing lives today. There are approximately 227 Names for Jesus in the Old Testament and the New Testament. He is the Second Adam and our Advocate, He is the Shepherd of Souls and the Lord of Glory, He is The Rose of Sharon and The Word of Life, He is Emmanuel and The Good Master, He is Faithful and True and the Prince of Life, He is our Chief Shepherd and The Captain of our Salvation. Jesus is many things to many men but the bottom line is – He is the Son of the True and Living God. He is One with the One that sits on the Throne. He is our God and our friend.

John 1:1-2
In the beginning was the Word, and the Word was with God, and the Word was God. He was in the beginning with God. All things were made through Him, and without Him nothing was made that was made.

First of all, we cannot ascertain what the beginning is. Time from God's point of view and time from our point of view are entirely two different views. God always was and God always is, and God will forevermore be, this is what we know or should know. God is endless and timeless and we don't have a clue about anything unless He reveals it to us.

Jesus is the Word and Jesus was with God in the beginning. This means that God and Jesus had and have a timeless face to face relationship. Even though Jesus was in the beginning with God, God was still before Jesus before our time began. Even though Jesus and God are two different personalities, they are still One and the same. God the Father, God the Son, and God the Holy Spirit are all God.

Colossians 1:15-17
He (Jesus) is the image of the invisible God, the firstborn of all creation. For by Him all things were created that are in heaven and that are on the earth, visible and invisible, whether thrones or dominions or principalities or powers. All things

80

were created through Him and for Him. He is before all things, and in Him all things consist.

Jesus is the firstborn of all creation, not created, not fashioned, or shaped into being; He is the first born before there was a Heaven. Jesus was born - everything else and everyone else is created. Jesus created the angelic beings, the celestial creatures and all of the terrestrial creatures. Jesus created all the governmental facets of Heaven called principalities, powers, and rulers. He set spiritual laws in motion, He caused gravity to exist, He caused seed-time and harvest to exist, He caused every single-celled organism to exist, He caused every mammal, every amphibian, every reptile, every bird, and every creeping thing to exist. He created the life cycle and the food chain. From plants to trees, from valleys to mountains, from inner space to outer space, Jesus is the architect of this universe, of this planet, and of man.

God is sovereign and in His sovereignty He knows everything. God knew that Adam would fall and cause every man after him to live in a fallen state of life. God knew that Satan and his demons would enslave millions of people in Skotos or darkness. He knew His creation would be literally living in spiritual, moral, and intellectual darkness. God knew that people would live in error, ignorance, disobedience, willful blindness and would rebel against the truth of His Word. Even though we treated God badly by living badly, He always had a plan for our salvation.

When the four-hundred years of silence from Heaven had ended, or when the fullness of time had come. I believe that God the Father looked to His Son and told Him to start fulfilling the Scriptures He (Jesus) had prophesied to His kings, Priest and Prophets for the past four-thousand years. So Jesus sent His angel to Zacharias to announce the birth of John the Baptist who would be in the spirit and power of Elijah. Six months later, He sent Gabriel to a young woman that He chose to be His virgin mother, and blessed her and made her highly favored, to announce the preparations of His birth. A plethora of events were set in motion so that the Scriptures would be fulfilled in Christ Jesus our Lord. When King Herod heard of the new king born in Bethlehem he ordered all the two year old males to be murdered in an attempt to retain his position. From the shepherds and wise men to the census that cause the population explosion to overrun Bethlehem; the Jesus prophesies were coming to pass. From the town of Bethlehem to Calvary to resurrection Sunday, over three-hundred Scriptures would come to pass and the people of the earth would have a chance to receive genuine salvation.

In Him was life, and the life was the light of men.

As the song goes, *'He came from Heaven to earth to show us the way'*. He would sit and dine with tax collectors, prostitutes, murderers, thieves, liars and sinners in general to show them that there is a better way to live. That His yoke was easy and His burden is light. That He was the good shepherd and He came *to give us life and life more abundantly*. He told them to come to Him so that they may find rest. Many believed in Him and were happy; they were astonished, and marveled at the miracles He performed before their eyes, the healing of the sick, the raising the dead, and the words that flowed from His lips brought life and light to the ones that were living in darkness.

John 1:5
And the light shines in the darkness, and the darkness did not comprehend it.

It is impossible for darkness to comprehend light. They are enmity with each other. Some folk say that opposites attract, but that will never be the case in the subject matter here. The darkness will never understand, grasp, fathom or cognize the light.

Jesus is the true Light that shows each and every man, woman and child that had been living in darkness and that God has sent Him into the world to bring light, to bring clarity of life, to bring peace, to bring healing, to bring deliverance, to bring salvation, to bring the Truth. There are a lot of good people in the world, those who do great deeds for others, but these good people cannot save themselves nor can they place themselves in Heaven for good works or hell for missing the mark. Faith in Christ is a darkness buster, because once Jesus exposes the darkness in us, we find that we have been living in vain because we were actually living in darkness trying to represent the light.

v 10
He came to His own, and His own did not know Him.

Jesus, the creator of the heavens and earth and made man in His imagine did not know Him when He came to His creation. People were in the habit of living in the darkness, they were unable to know Christ unless it was by divine revelation.

This is like a person who has been in prison for several years without any contact with anyone. Then the warden comes along with release papers but the person refuses freedom because he/she did not know what it was. He/she had grown accustomed or was comfortable in the darkness of prison and it became such a way of life, which in his mind, there was no other way to live. The person did not comprehend, realize, grasp, or understand the fact that life and freedom was in the possession of the warden. And because the person did not know who this bearer of freedom was, they refused. Jesus came to His own people, His own creation and they did not know Him. They read about Him in the Scriptures and were waiting for Him – but they did not know Him when He got there.

He came to give us life but we couldn't understand it. Can you imagine looking at yourself in a mirror and don't know who you are. Darkness and unsound judgment will always go hand in hand. There are a lot of people that do not like change in their lives. There are a lot of people that are comfortable with the way they live. There are a lot of people that are content with a little sin here and a little sin there in their lives. As long as the bills are paid, the lights are on, the cable is functioning and there is food on the table, people are happy and call themselves blessed. People love a variety of things and they want to make their own choices on how they want to live. Generally, when something new comes around, (an idea or new way of living), people do not understand – they will most likely kill what they don't understand. For these reasons, Jesus was rejected by most. They would rather walk in the mud and mire of darkness than to walk in the light of His Word.

vs 12-13
But as many as received Him, to them He gave the right to become children of God, to those who believe in His name: who were born, not of blood, nor of the will of the flesh, nor of the will of man, but of God.

Some did not believe in Him as the Son of God, and yet some did. But those that believed in Him were granted the right to be sons and daughters of God. This is a legal right. An example of this is when a person turns 16 years of age, they may take a drivers' test and if they passed the test they had a right to drive a car. When we received Jesus, God gave us the legal right to become children of God. When we believe in His Name, we are born-again – born of God. Our belief system changed from the darkness to the light, and then the Holy Spirit develops us into the reality of new creatures in Christ Jesus. In Christ old things (darkness) have passed away and behold, all things (light) become new.

This is a spiritual truth – if we are born once, we will die twice; but if we are born twice – we will only die once. Being born once is from the flesh (our mothers). But our second birth comes from God and we have passed from death into life.

And the Word became flesh and dwelt among us, and we beheld His glory, the glory as of the only begotten of the Father, full of grace and truth

The Word became flesh, or Jesus laid down His Godly power and became a man. He lived as man in the midst of men, however; He was no ordinary man. It must have been wonderful to have that revelation of Jesus Christ as a man when men beheld, observed, and witnessed His glory. The glory as the only begotten of God, full of grace (God's unmerited favor and God's divine influence upon the hearts of men), and full of truth.

> *Philippians 2:5-8*
> *Let this mind be in you which was also in Christ Jesus, who being in the form of God, did not consider it robbery to be equal with God, but made Himself of no reputation, taking the form of a bond servant, and coming in the likeness of men. And being found in the appearance as a man, He humbled Himself and became obedient to the point of death, even the death of the cross.*

Jesus did not consider it a big thing to lose His All Seeing, All Knowing, All Powerful status. He knew that He would come to Earth as a man, redeem mankind and return to His place on the Throne and the right hand of God. He knew that He had to humble Himself as a man, in the appearance of a man to give the world a second chance.

The Works of Christ

Now the first sign or miracle that Jesus performed was in the town of Cana where a wedding took place. I don't believe that I have met anyone who does not know this story. Even comedians have made comments about Jesus turning water into wine. There are many people who do not believe in drinking wine but there are also many who do believe that we can consume wine. The bottom line is that Jesus came to do good works and show us the way to salvation. Whether we drink wine or not shouldn't be the topic of debate. Our main concern as a Christian is to be obedient to God and to allow the Holy Spirit to work through us.

When Jesus returned from the wilderness where He was tested for forty days and forty nights by the devil, He went to Galilee in the power of the Spirit and the news of Him spread all across the surrounding region. He began teaching in their synagogues and was glorified by all. He picked up the scroll and went to *Isaiah 61:1-2* and read,

Luke 4:18

"The Spirit of the Lord is upon Me, because He has anointed Me to preach the gospel to the poor; He has sent Me to heal the brokenhearted, to proclaim liberty to the captives and recovery of sight to the blind, to set at liberty those who are oppressed; To proclaim the acceptable year of the Lord."

When He had finished reading, the crowd looked at Him closely and Jesus said to them, *"Today this scripture is fulfilled in your hearing."* The crowd marveled at the gracious Words that fell from His lips, but just like the first seed in the parable of the sower, doubt crept in and they said, *"Is this not Joseph's son?"* The kingdom of darkness will not relent in its pursuit of rebellion against God and His Christ.

I want you to notice the language here in *Isaiah 61:1-2* and *Luke 4:18*.

"The Spirit of the Lord is upon Me, because He has anointed Me to preach the gospel to the poor..."

God anointed Jesus to do the works that God wanted Him to do. 'Jesus was to preach the Gospel to the poor', to tell of God's salvation plan to the deprived, unfortunate, underprivileged, and the meager. Those who aren't so religious-minded, rule minded, tradition minded, it renders, reduces, and condenses them of no earthly good. Jesus did not come for the religious because they thought and believed they were just fine and didn't need any help. They had put God in a box and were lord over their own lives. Jesus said I did not come for the righteous but for the unrighteous or sinners. He came to a people that had no hope and was in despair, misery, anguish, and gloom.

He has sent Me to heal the brokenhearted, to proclaim liberty to the captives and recovery of sight to the blind, to set at liberty those who are oppressed;

The activities of the day were horrid and nasty, callous, vile and mean to those that were without any social standing. The religious sects of the day did not have a heart or empathy for the less fortunate. Also, there were not any hospitals, urgent care centers, or counselors that were available to the lower class citizens. But God sent Jesus to heal the broken hearted, to proclaim liberty and freedom to a society that was bogged down in the mire where life was hard and meaningless.

God sent Jesus from Heaven to Earth to give sight to the blind and not only physical sight, but spiritual sight to those who wanted escape from the kingdom of darkness. His assignment from the Almighty Father was to free us from ourselves, and free us from the devil and his demons to a life that would be pleasing to God. All of this sounds great but there are some folk who were just plain hardheaded and did not heed the Word of the Lord. So everyone was not convinced that Jesus was who He said He was.

> *Luke 4:24-27*
> *Then Jesus said, "Assuredly, I say to you, no prophet is accepted in his own country. But I tell you truly, many widows were in Israel in the days of Elijah, when the heaven was shut up three years and six months, and there was great famine throughout all the land; but to none of them was Elijah sent except to Zarephath, in the region of Sidon, to a woman who was a widow. And many lepers were in Israel in this time of Elisha the prophet, and none of them was cleansed except Naaman the Syrian.*

When Jesus said these things, the people were full of wrath because he told the truth about them and their ancient relatives from centuries past. That in the days of Elijah and Elisha, God spent His healing power on people who were not children of the covenant. They wanted to kill Him right then and there because they were insulted and they took Jesus to the crest of the hill to throw Him over the cliff. But Jesus just walked through the crowd and suffered no harm.

The spirit of religion is a very strong spirit. It feeds and lives on offense and pride; we have found that it is alive and well all over the world today. It is set in its ways and will not bulge because in these cults, they believe that they know it all and they are the upper echelon in spiritual matters. The people in the above Scripture marveled at the Words of Jesus, but when He told the truth about their ancestors, their admiration quickly curdled and of the grace that fell from His lips, soured and turned the offended group into a lynch mob with intentions to kill the One they had admired only moments ago.

Jesus left Galilee and went to Capernaum, and as was His custom, He taught on the Sabbath in the synagogue. The people were also astonished by the teaching of the Master because He taught with authority. There was a man with an unclean demon in the synagogue that day and he said with a loud voice, "Let us alone! What have we to do with You, Jesus of Nazareth? Did you come to destroy us? I know who You are – the Holy One of God!" When the demon spoke out, Jesus told him to be quiet or shut up. Again demons recognize Jesus, they know Who He is. Demons and devils know their future but they keep attempting to cause the people on the earth to rebel with them against God.

> *After Jesus rebuked the demon and cast him out of the man, the people were once again amazed, this time at what they witnessed and said among themselves:*
> *For with authority and power He commands the unclean spirits, and they come out. And the report about Him went out into every place in the surrounding region.*
> *Then Jesus left the synagogue and went to Peter's house and found Peter's mother-in-law sick with high fever. Jesus rebuked the fever and she got up and served Him. The news of the works of Jesus had gone out and by sundown – all who were sick, all who were afflicted, all who had diseases and all who were possessed by demons came to Jesus and were healed and delivered.*

Jesus started in the synagogue quoting Isaiah and told them this Scripture is fulfilled in their hearing. Then He proved it by healing all the people that were sick and afflicted, and possessed to confirm what He said was true. Most believed Him and some did not know what to think. However, Jesus did not rely on what people thought, He went about His Father's business and to do the mission God had ordained Him to do.

A Lesson from Christ

In The *Book of Luke 5*, we find a very valuable lesson in obedience. Jesus was teaching the multitude by the Lake of Gennesaret.   There were so many people there, they pressed against Him as He taught the word. Jesus looked around and saw two boats aground and empty because the fishermen were cleaning their nets. So He got into the boat, which belonged to Simon Peter, and told him to cast it out into the water. Simon did so and Jesus taught from there.

When He had finished the lesson, He told Peter, "Launch out into the deep and let down your nets for a catch."

But Simon Peter answered Him, "Master, we have toiled all night and caught nothing; nevertheless at Your word I will let down the net." And when they had let down their net, they caught a great number of fish, and their net was breaking. So Peter called his partners, (James and John), over to help them with the great number of fish and when they came, the bounty filled both boats with so many fish that they began to sink. Then Peter realized what had happened and fell to his knees at the feet of Jesus and said, "Depart from me, for I am a sinful man, Oh Lord."

Jesus had a system, if I dare to say that. The pattern is that after He preached, He performed miracles. Faith comes by hearing and hearing by the Word of God. Whenever the Word of God is preached, faith ignites in our spirits and it boosts our belief system. When our belief receives this boost our faith becomes stronger, and when our faith becomes strong – we believe we receive.

Jesus told Peter to go out into the deep and drop down your nets (plural). First, Peter told Jesus there were no fish out there. They had toiled, labored, and slogged all night and they did not catch a single fish. There are a lot of times when the Spirit urges us to do something that is beyond our capacity to grasp, so we make excuses. We say some pretty silly stuff like, "Lord I have been trying all day or all night to do this and it just won't happen. Lord I tried. Lord I can't or Lord they keep…" Excuses are not of God and since we are children of God – excuses should be far from us.

This moment of lapsing in belief is a common trait to men. Abraham went through it when he told the king that his wife was his sister out of fear. Gideon did not have a high opinion of himself and thought that he could not win the war. Elijah allowed a woman to run him out of town after he killed 450 prophets of Baal. So sometimes we are prone to stumble when it comes to the Word of God.

"Master, we have toiled all night and caught nothing; nevertheless at Your Word I will let down the net." Peter tried to make his case but something happened within and he said, *"Nevertheless – at Your Word!"* Peter shifted gears; *"So what, we have toiled all night! So what, we have labored in vain, so what! Nevertheless, at Your Word."* It seemed that Peter was working on a revelation and did not know it. And the bottom line was Jesus told him to do it, he did it and the results were overwhelming. Jesus told him to throw out his nets, but Peter only threw one net and the one net could not hold the miracle of the great multitude of fish. In fact, it almost sunk his boat and his partner's boat. If he had thrown out more than one net as Jesus said, they would not have struggled so much with the catch of fish. That is a lesson within itself.

Obedience to the Word is a character trait of the Kingdom of God. At Your Word, or because You say so Jesus, I know I will be successful in this endeavor, in this trial, or in this storm. Now Peter was expecting results, but he was not expecting the over-abundance of fish that was so overwhelming he fell at the feet of Jesus and confessed that he was a sinful man. This is the first sign of repentance – knowing that you are a sinner and in need a Savior.

Today, we have the Bible; we have the Holy Spirit dwelling in us. The rules have not changed, we still need to be obedient to the Word, we still need to follow instructions, and we still need to be faithful.

Declaration

My faith works
I always have a good report
I am on God's side and He is on my side
I belong to God and I serve God
I am a child of God
I believe God that it shall be even
As it was told me in His Holy Word
God's Word cannot fail and I cannot fail
I am standing on the Word
I am standing on the His promises

Notes:

Notes:

Chapter 7

Hearing from Heaven

Whose Your Daddy

Four hundred years after God's rebuke in *Malachi,* our spiritual situation as mankind had gotten worse. In the eighth chapter of *The Book of John*, we find an interesting conversation between Jesus and the Pharisees. The story starts with a woman caught in adultery. I personally believe the religious leaders paid the woman to have sex with the man and then busted her to expose her. The Jews had a history of hiring people/false witnesses to fit their agenda. They also had the habit of buying false witnesses. They did it at the trial of Jesus. They hired witnesses at the killing of Stephen; they had false witnesses at Paul's trial. Therefore, I believe they hired a man to engage in sex with the married woman and watched them through the widow. "Caught in the very act!" The Bible says Satan is the accuser of the brethren, and we can see his hand was in this mess. They really did not care about the woman, the man or the act – they wanted trap Jesus into saying something contrary to the Law of Moses or out of context with the Word of God. They have been plotting to kill Him since He gave the discourse on Elijah and Elisha healing Gentiles in *Luke 4.*

They had their plan in place and they thought they had Him. However, they never saw His answer coming, *"He who is without sin, cast the first stone."* Darkness was caught off guard. They were frozen like a deer in the headlights of an on-coming car. They started thinking on all the sins they had committed throughout their lives. And for some, the sin they were committing now. So one by one, they threw down their instruments of death and walked away, starting with the oldest for he was certainly convicted of the many sins he had committed in his lifetime to the youngest and all the sins he also remembered committing.

I know that you are Abraham's descendants, but you seek to kill Me, because My word has no place in you. I speak what I have seen with My father; and you do what you have seen with your father."

The darkness had the Jews thinking they had salvation through the physical seed of Abraham. They believed it was their birthright to Heaven. They had no idea that it would require a spiritual rebirth from the natural to the spiritual.

They sought to kill Jesus and in that alone proved they were living in darkness and could not be a son of Abraham in spirit. Abraham did not have a murderous heart. Jesus was about to give them the lesson of, "Like father like son". As Satan was and is a murderer, the sons of darkness are also murderers at heart. Jesus told them they wanted to kill Him because the Word of life had no place in them. The Word was a foreign language to them, and they could not comprehend. This is like staring at a coffee table for several hours and can't comprehend that it's a coffee table. They were so full of darkness the light of Christ was vacant in their hearts and they could not partake in any understanding of spiritual matters. Clarity, lucidity, or transparency will never be an attribute in the kingdom of darkness.

They answered and said to Him, "Abraham is our father." Jesus said to them, "if you were Abraham's children, you would do the works of Abraham. But you seek to kill Me, a Man who has told you the truth which I heard from God. Abraham did not do this.

Jesus had a habit of calling it like it is. He told them just because they are Abraham's descendants by the flesh, they were still the sons of the devil by the spirit. The evidence that they were not the sons of Abraham was in their actions. Abraham did not have a murderous heart. He was meek and mild yet powerful in the Lord. This is because he fully trusted God and was fully persuaded that God is the answer to all things. The religious sect of that day did not trust God as Abraham did and they relied fully on themselves for they were self-made men. Jesus was clearly showing them the difference between the works of God and the works of the devil.

"You do the deeds of your father." Then they said to Him, "We were not born of fornication; we have one father – God.

Still, the Jews were hanging onto their birthright.

Jesus said to them, If God were your Father, you would love Me, for I proceeded forth and came from God; nor have I come of Myself, but He sent Me.

As God loves, so we should love. The children of God should love as God loves. Jesus was telling these men that if God were their Father then they would act like the Father. Once again, they were giving lip service because they had no love for Jesus and their actions supported this. Jesus was pointing out that if you loved the Father you would love the Son.

He went a step further and told them that God had sent Him to the earth to save those who did not love Him. Jesus said that He proceed forth from God, as if God pulled Him out of His bosom. Jesus was to show the religious system of the day the correct way of righteousness and the correct way of serving the Father. Jesus was saying, "Hey! I am here to represent God! I am here to show you the way to the Father!"

The religious sect truly thought they were doing the will of God, when in essence; they were doing the work of the darkness. As mentioned before, with darkness come deceit, ignorance and confusion. This is clearly seen in this discourse.

If this religious sect were of God, they would have loved Jesus and the work He was doing. But they actually hated Him because

His works were unexplainable and they didn't have the knowledge of how to perform miracles as Jesus did. They were actually jealous of Him. They were also indignant because He healed people on the Sabbath while demanding respect for the Temple of God. This is a common trait of the offense folks take when they are doing wrong and someone points it out. *The Book of Proverbs* has plenty to say about correcting a fool and mockers.

> *Proverbs 9:7*
> *Do not correct a scoffer, lest he hates you; rebuke a wise man and he will love you.*

> *Proverbs 12:15*
> *The way of a fool is right in his own eyes, but he who heeds wise counsel is wise.*

> *Proverbs 14:6*
> *A scoffer seeks wisdom and does not find it, but knowledge is easy to him who understands.*

> *Proverbs 15:12*
> *A Scoffer does not love one who corrects him, nor will he go to the wise.*

To make matters worse, Jesus told them He came from God; the religious sect were under the impression He came from Nazareth. They knew His parents and probably watched Him grow up. At the age of twelve He caused them to be astonished with the understanding He possessed. But here, they were mistaken and had no understanding of His identity and they couldn't dispute the miracles of healing and the feeding the multitudes. They felt they should be the ones with this power. They felt they had arrived and had been placed above all the common folk, including Jesus. But Jesus threw a monkey wrench in the stew and there was nothing they could do about it. Then to top it all off, Jesus calls them sons of devils.

Why do you not understand My speech? Because you are not able to listen to My Word.

These men were natural men and natural men cannot understand anything spiritual. Without the Spirit of God, a man cannot even begin to comprehend the things of God. So the more Jesus talked the less they understood. This was probably very frustrating to the religious sect and it fueled their anger even more with the Son of Man.

1 Corinthians 2:14
But the natural man does not receive the things of the Spirit of God, for they are foolishness to him; nor can he know them, because they are spiritually discerned.

Jesus told them they were unable to understand His Words. Snakes cannot fly, sharks cannot walk, the fragrance of skunks will never be used to sell as perfume, and people under the influence of darkness will never understand the light.

You are of your father the devil, and the desires of your father you want to do. He was a murderer from the beginning, and does not stand in the truth, because there is no truth in him. When he speaks a lie, he speaks from his own resources, for he is a liar and the father of it.

Like father, like son. They became sons of Satan by not believing in Jesus as the Christ, the Holy Son of God. Sons inherent their characteristics from their father, hence, the apple doesn't fall too far from the tree. The religious sect had solidified their allegiance, loyalty and commitment to the devil due to their unwillingness to accept Jesus as the Christ. When a person rejects the truth, the void within them will be filled with lies. Deceit and lies is a pair of dominant forces in the kingdom of darkness where the truth is neither welcome nor desired. Just as truth, mercy and love are the fruit of Heaven; lies, hatred, and deceit are the natural resources in the kingdom of Satan, the kingdom of darkness.

Because I tell you the truth, you do not believe Me. Which of you convicts Me of sin? And if I tell the truth, why do you not believe Me?

When I was lost, I hated it when someone was telling me the truth about me. It was something that I didn't want to hear. So I understand how the Pharisees felt when Jesus reprimanded them with the knowledge about themselves. They knew He was right and they hated Him for it.

Jesus asked which one of you can convict me of sin. They could not answer that question because Jesus did not commit any sin. The religious leaders had been sending spies to try and catch Him committing a sin but they were without success. And because of this, He made this special group all the more furious. They were so infuriated with Him that they were unable to hear the truth.

John 8:47
He who is of God hears God's words; therefore you do not hear, because you are not of God.

Whoever believes in God has the ability to hear His Words. If the Bible speaks to you by the Spirit when you read it, then you are hearing God's Word. If the Spirit is not speaking to you then you are not of God. For example, when I was lost, I tried reading the Bible but I didn't understand what I was reading. I was seeing the Words, pronouncing the words, but they had no meaning for me. There was no illumination, no revelation or understanding in the Words of the Book. But when I was born-again, the scales that covered my eyes were removed and I could hear and understand what the Word was telling me. I guess you could call it a moment of clarity, a moment of lucidity, and clearness. I was sober because I was born-again. But the fact of the matter is that God opened my ears so that I could hear, He opened my eyes so that I could see. He did this based on the decision I wanted Jesus in my life to reign and rule. As I said earlier, it was so wonderful to me that I stayed in the Word, reading the Word, and soaking up the Word for upwards of ten to twelve hours a day. I was like a sponge, soaking the truth at every opportunity. I loved it and I could not get enough of it. The Word brings life and the only way you can understand God, is to be of God. You can only be of God, if you believe God.

It is a terrible thing to disbelieve God. When a person does not believe God, he cannot have any part of God nor any of the good things that He has for us. Furthermore, a person in this condition will not be able to see truth in any spiritual matter. He will try to explain the things of God and the ways of God with a carnal mind and that is impossible. He will certainly be a naysayer and will not be able to see any good in anyone or anything.

Jesus is telling us here that not only were the Pharisees and Sadducees were blind, but they were also false teachers. A false teacher is one who does not hold to the doctrine of God and Christ. A false teacher is one who preaches from his flesh and has not been indoctrinated by God. When a false teacher teaches, he is polluting the souls of the people because he does not have the wisdom of God in him or on him. He is robbing the people of the truth and possibly, eternal life.

Prayer

Most gracious Heavenly Father, I bow my knees to You, God and Father of my Lord and Savior Jesus Christ, from Whom the whole family in Heaven and on earth is named, that You would grant me , according to the riches of Your glory, that I may be strengthened with might through Your Spirit in my inner man, so that Christ may dwell in my heart through faith; and that I am being rooted and grounded in love, so that I may be able to comprehend with all the saints, what is the width and length and depth and height – and to know the love of Christ which passes all understanding and knowledge; so that I may be filled with all the fullness of God.

Father, I know that you are able to do exceedingly, abundant-

ly above all that I can ask or think, according to the power that works in me, I give You all the praise and glory and honor to the King of kings and the Lord of lords, for all You have done I in my life. In Jesus Name, Amen

Notes:

Chapter 8

Sowing and Reaping

The Process of the Seed

Jesus shows us Kingdom traits through the parables He taught to His disciples. The following parables of the Kingdom of God/Heaven, or God's way of doing things, will deal with seed, which is a part of sowing and reaping.

> *Mark 4:26-27*
> *And He said, "The kingdom of God is as if a man should scatter seed on the ground, and should sleep by night and rise by day, and the seed should sprout and grow, he himself does not know how.*

Jesus taught in parables and in these parables, He used terms that were common to men in those days. Farming was a trade most of the population of Israel was accustomed to because just about everyone grew something from dates, to wheat, to grapes. They had knowledge of planting and harvesting. So He taught in terms they could understand.

When a farmer scatters seed, he leaves it in the ground. He covers the seed with the earth and waters it and then he waits. He has faith that the seed he planted will grow into a plant and will produce the desired affect he envisioned. Notice the farmer doesn't go back to the spot and dig up the seed to see if it was doing what he set it there to do. However, he tends and cares for it, and he keeps the weeds away from the plant so they don't choke his crop. He doesn't know the mechanics of how the seed grows but he waits until the plant develops into maturity till harvest time.

Mark 4:28-29

For the earth yields crops by itself: first the blade, then the head, after that the full grain in the head. But when the grain ripens, immediately he puts the sickle, because the harvest has come.

Jesus says that the earth yields the crops by itself. In Genesis One, God said to be fruitful and multiply. Every seed bearing plant will grow, scatter seed and the process repeats itself over and over for years to come.

The seed stories are examples of the spiritual law of reaping what you sow. In *Galatians 6:7-8*, Paul gives us the bottom line about life,

"Do not be deceived, God is not mocked: for whatever a man sows that he will also reap. For he who sows to his flesh will of the flesh reap corruption, but he who sows to the Spirit will of the Spirit reap everlasting life."

Sowing and reaping works like this: when a man sows into something, he is giving. It could be money, time, love, peace, joy, gentleness, goodness, faithfulness, meekness, or a smile. Sowing is an action. It is something you do. Just like the farmer would sow a seed into the ground then the ground would yielded a crop. Whether its apples, wheat, corn, cotton, soybeans or whatever. What he sows is what he will reap. When you sow love into the life of someone, you will reap love. It doesn't necessarily mean you will reap from the same person you sow into. When you sow money, you will reap money, but not necessarily from the same person you sowed money into. Reaping can come from people you don't even know. Sometimes, God will send a person form Africa, or the west coast or England or anywhere from the four corners of the earth to come and bless you.

When you sow your time with the Father, you will reap the benefits of the Father. You will develop His characteristics, His wisdom, His ways, and His love. However, if you sow to the world, you will reap the ways of the world. If you sow your time in television watching, you will reap the characteristics of what you watch on television.

I am not saying that television is bad, but most of shows and com-mercials on television could dilute the Christians' spirit, because it sows the thoughts of the world's system into the viewer's mind. So if you sow most of your time in beer commercials, or shows with strong sexual content, or violent content, then you will eventually act these things out. The seed here is the thought and thoughts lead to action. If you sow into crime, you will reap the rewards of crime, which is personal destruction. If you sow hatred, you will reap ha-tred. If you sow discord, you will reap discord. However, if you sow love, you will reap love. If you sow kindness, you will reap kindness. *God is not mocked;* you will reap what you sow.

In the Kingdom of God, Jesus is the seed the Christian sows. To sow is to give something. As the farmer plants a seed in the ground, we are to plant the Word of God in the hearts of men and women who do not know Him. Our number one priority is to spread the Gospel of the risen Lord Jesus, God's Christ. We are to seek and save those who do not know the way. We are to feed the sheep, and take care of the Lambs. We are to convince by our lifestyles there is a better way to live, a way that is powerful, blessed, victorious, and knowledgeable. A way of life that is ordained by God and empowered by God's Holy Spirit and consummated by the blood of the Lamb.

God is telling us to sow our time, our money, our efforts into spiritual things and we will reap what we have sown. We don't have to die to have a good life. However, we need to die daily to the ways of society or the world. Jesus tells us we will reap life and life more abundantly here on earth.

Seed can be sown in a number of ways. Other than preaching or proclaiming the Word of God, we can sow seeds in our actions such as a friendly smile, or a kind word. Basic love for our fellow man can win someone to the Lord. One day a man came to our service who had been into all types of religions from Islam to Wicca. But brotherly love and kindness was sown into his life by the character of Jesus won this man to Christ. About five or six years ago, another man who was bound in Islam loved to sing. I had formed a praise team and we were in the middle of practice preparing for a revival.

He came in and asked if he could sing with us, I told him that we were singing about the love of Jesus. He said okay and within a few months, he gave his life to Christ.

We can also plant seeds into someone's life through material things such as money, cars, houses, business, and land. Covenant teacher Mitch Mullin often looks for homeless people on the road to sow into. Some of these men may be drug addicts or alcoholics, or they could just be running game, but when you sow into them in the attitude of the love of Christ, the Holy Ghost is all over that money and miracles happen. He sows in a position of strength, knowing that the Holy Ghost can override any addiction. This same thing happened in *The Book of Acts* when *God worked unusual miracles by the hand of Paul so that even handkerchiefs or aprons were brought from Paul's His body to the sick, and the diseases left them and evil spirits went out of them.* [See *Acts 19:11-12*] Nothing is impossible for God.

The Best Seed

God set the standard in sowing and reaping. He set this standard when He sowed His Son into this lost and dying world to die for us. His Son represents the seed. God sowed Jesus into the earth to reap Sons of God.

> *John 12:24*
> *Most assuredly, I say to you, unless a grain of wheat falls into the ground and dies, it remains alone; but if it dies, it produces much grain, (Fruit)*

Jesus was that seed of grain that fell to the earth and died for our sins, our sickness, our diseases, our hurts, our pains, our ignorance in spiritual things, our wayward ways, our hard hearts, our fallacies, and our lives of living in darkness. He did this so that all the people who believe that Jesus is the Son of God can be reconciled or reaped back to Him.

When God raised Jesus from the dead, we became the fruit of His actions. One-grain head can produce thousands, if not millions of more grain. When Jesus died and went into the tomb as a seed, He gave life to millions of people. He gained or produced much fruit.

> *John 3:16-17*
> *"For God so loved the world that He gave His only begotten Son, that whoever believes in Him should not perish but have everlasting life. For God did not send His Son into the world to condemn the world but that the world through Him might be saved."*

In *Romans 6*, the Holy Spirit penned through the Apostle Paul reveals that when Jesus was baptized into death, submerged into the earth, we were also baptized into death. This was God's plan all along. And since He raised Jesus from the dead, we were also raised with Him and are now able to walk in the newness of life. This newness of life is the complete opposite of what we used to be.

If a man planted apple seeds, then apple trees would be the products of the harvest. Since we were united in Christ in the likeness of His death, we were also beautified in the likeness of His resurrection.

Our old man represents the seed that went into the ground, and the new man emerged from the ground. Our sin nature died in that ground and the yoke of sin became a dead issue in the life of the newly raised man or woman of God. We were buried as sinners but were resurrected as sons and daughters in the Kingdom of God.

Since we have died, then death cannot have any dominion, jurisdiction, reign, supremacy, sway, control, or mastership over us. We have the power to do the right thing because we are no longer slaves to what we don't want to do. So now we are to consider ourselves to be dead in sin and alive to God in Christ Jesus, and the rest of our lives are dedicated to do the works of righteousness by the power of God.

The Kingdom of God/Heaven is a spiritual reality to each person who receives Jesus Christ as Lord and Savior. It is not just a nice thought or a marvelous idea; it is a real life for the man or woman of faith. When we, like the seed that died and was buried but came to life through God's process, we are transferred from the kingdom of darkness to the Kingdom of Light or the Kingdom of God. *Colossians 1:13-14* tells us,

> *"He has delivered us from the power of darkness and conveyed us into the kingdom of the Son of His love, in whom we have redemption through His blood, the forgiveness of sins."*

Conveyed means, 'transferred.' So in essence, those who are in Christ have been transferred from Satan's kingdom into the Kingdom of God, or God's way of doing things. This transfer happens on the inside of man. In his spirit which is the real you.

Notes:

Chapter 9
Speaking in Parables *(Part 1)*

Parables

One day Jesus went to the beach and sat down. After a while, a great number of people came and gathered around Him. They were hungry for the phenomenon that was shaking up the region and would soon shake up the world. Some had witnessed His miracles while others only heard of them, they were anxious to see what this man of God would do next. They were anxious to hear what He had to say. These people did not understand exactly what He was saying, but His language was uplifting and different from anything they've ever heard. He spoke with authority and power that surpassed everything they ever heard. When the crowd grew too huge for Him to stand on the beach, He got into a nearby boat and taught on the Kingdom of God while the people stood on the beach and listened.

After the sermon, the disciples came to Him and asked Him why did He teach in parables? No one could understand what He was talking about. Jesus answered saying that:

Because it has been given to you to know the mysteries of the Kingdom of Heaven but to them it has not been given.

About a third of the teachings of Jesus were taught in parables. A parable is a brief story, to teach a point or an analogy to illustrate spiritual truths. It is like a riddle or an enigma declaring a truth. Most of the teachings of Christ were straight and to the point, but some teachings were parables. *The parable of the sower* is probably the most famous analogies; and the Lord said if you understand this parable, you would be able to understand all parables.

God chose all twelve disciples for a specific purpose. In verse 11, Jesus told them they essentially had favor with God because they were granted to know secrets of the Kingdom while everyone else will not be granted insight on the Kingdom at that particular time.

Therefore I speak to them in parables, because seeing they do not see, and hearing they do not hear, nor do they understand.

I imagine this would be like hearing words in your native language but cannot comprehend what is said because it sounds like a foreign language. This is a prime example of the carnal mind unable to comprehend spiritual truths.

Every week thousands flock to the church houses across the United States and hear preaching or teaching. However, most will not remember the topic of the sermon three hours later. I believe that most people hear the tone of the message, the highs and lows, but miss the message itself. Emotionalism has played a colossal part in the churches across the United States today, but when the congregation comes down from their emotional high, they find themselves in the same condition they were in before they went.

These temporary fixes have become common place for most folks. When things become common place then one would grow dull in hearing. It is not just the congregations; some pastors of these churches also play a crucial part in that they cater to the emotions of their flock.

The Parable of the Ten Virgins

Then the kingdom of heaven shall be liken to ten virgins who took their lamps and went out to meet the bridegroom. Now five of them were wise and five were foolish. Those who were foolish took their lamps and took no oil with them, But the wise took oil in their vessels with their lamps. But while the bridegroom was delayed, they all slumbered and slept. And at midnight a cry was heard: Behold, the bridegroom is coming;

go out to meet Him! Then all those virgins arose and trimmed their lamps. And the foolish said to the wise, "Give us some of your oil, for our lamps are going out." But the wise answered saying, "No lest there should not be enough for us and you; but go rather to those who sell, and buy for yourselves.

And while they went to buy, the bridegroom came, and those who were ready went in with him to the wedding; and the door was shut.

In the 25th chapter of Matthew, Jesus taught on the subject of His return via a parable entitled the Parable of the Ten Virgins. It is a startling parable that indicates that only half of the Church will be ready for His return.

The first question that comes to mind is how in the world is only half the Church saved? There are two types of churches in this world. The first Church is the Church that keeps their eyes on God. This is the Church that is alert and sensitive to the voice of God. This is the Church that has a relationship with God the Father, God the Son, and God the Holy Spirit. This is the Church that is led by the Spirit of God and is also a doer of the Word of God. The mentality of this Church is God comes first; and the lambs and sheep are fed the nourishment of His Word. The goals of the Church are the same as God's goals. The attitude of this Church is to hate evil, to be unspotted from the world, to pray for her enemies, to carry out the great commission, and to love one another.

The other church is the church that mixes the things of God with the things of the world. This church has self-appointed hirelings instead of ministers who are called by God. These men call themselves, anoint themselves, and ordain themselves, (or through the buddy system). The main focus of this particular church is based mainly on political issues instead of spiritual matters. This church is the church that caters to like-minded individuals, or specific social classes, instead of ministering to the needs of the downtrodden, the sick, the troubled, the lost, strangers, orphans and widows. This church is the church that preaches and teaches superficial substances instead of feeding the congregation true manna from the throne of God.

Then the kingdom of heaven shall be liken to ten virgins who took their lamps and went out to meet the bridegroom. Now five of them were wise and five were foolish.

I want you to notice all ten virgins received the invitation into the Kingdom. Many are called, but few are chosen. The chosen are the ones that have used what God has given them to advance the Kingdom in word and lifestyle. Five of these virgins were genuine converts and five were tares. Five are Kingdom of God-minded and five were the benefits of God-minded. There is nothing wrong with the benefits of God, and God promises us extraordinary benefits as children of the Kingdom. However, we as the Church should not just focus on the benefits in the Kingdom, we should also be aware of the fact that we are to pick up our cross daily and follow Him. Benefits come from obedience to His Word.

Genuine converts, the five wise virgins, are the ones that have received the gift of salvation with pure joy. True coverts are doers of the Word, and not hearers only. True converts are the ones that are submitted to God for His will to be done in their lives. The philosophy of the true convert equates that God is everything and the only thing we have to do with the world is to seek those in the world and show them God's salvation. The lives of genuine converts have truly changed and they want more of God than ever before, to spend their time with the Father and be involved in His will for their lives.

A false convert, the tares, or the five foolish virgins, just wants the benefits of the Kingdom without doing anything. This is sort of like welfare, receiving a check without doing any work system. Their idea of salvation is living as they want but collecting the benefits such as healing, deliverance, and all that goes with the new and better covenant that was provided through the blood of Jesus Christ. They fail to realize that He paid the ultimate price for our sins in order for us to walk in newness of life.

110

I need to make a point clear. These ten virgins have already confessed Jesus with their mouth but only five believed in their hearts. We cannot work our way into the Kingdom of God; but when we get in by faith – we have a job to do and that is being a witness for Christ. Salvation is a free gift to us. But after we received salvation we are not to sit on our blessed assurance and play around until Jesus returns.

We should be active members of Christ. Every member of the human body is active. Each member has its job to do. The heart pumps blood throughout the entire body. The lungs transfer oxygen to the blood and removes carbon dioxide from it. The kidneys filter liquid waste resulting from the metabolism of the blood and excrete it as urine. There are many parts and these parts work together to form a healthy functioning body.

The Church has many members and we all have a function in the body of Christ. It doesn't matter what it is; we should be active in the Church of the True and Living God. God calls us into our positions and we should work out our calling with the greatest of care. When we do, we'll be like the five wise virgins; we if we don't well…

Those who were foolish took their lamps and took no oil with them,

The lazy Christian wants everyone to help them, or do for them. The lazy Christian loves to just kick back and enjoy the benefits of Kingdom living, get fat and say 'God is good' and call themselves blessed. They often want the positions in the Church, such as Pastor, Teacher, Deacon, Praise Director, Usher, or some visible position in order to feel important and to be boss over others. Manipulation often comes with lazy Christians because it takes a plethora of excuses to get others to do what they should be doing for themselves and the Kingdom of God.

But the wise took oil in their vessels with their lamps.

Being prepared is always a plus in the physical world and also in the spiritual realm. For instance, if we know that we will be driving from Oklahoma City to Dallas today, we know that we need to make sure there is enough gas in the car, the tires have the right amount of air, and so on. As ministers of the Gospel, we are to stay ready to keep from getting ready. Our relationship with the Father should be a continual affair. The Word tells us to be ready in season and out and out of season. [See *2 Timothy 4:2*] We are subject to be called upon at any time. Sometimes, things happen and you don't have the time to get prayed up, or prepared in the spirit. You may have to act instantly because it may be the difference between life and death, either spiritually or physically.

When we look at the example of the Master, Jesus the Christ, we see that people would often come to Him at all times of the day and night. People came when it was convenient and when it wasn't. He didn't set appointments to heal people or to deliver them from their ailments. He was ready in season and out of season; He was ready all the time. As it was for the master, it is for us today. The five wise virgins were ready.

But while the bridegroom was delayed, they all slumbered and slept. And at midnight a cry was heard: Behold, the bridegroom is coming; go out to meet Him!

It has been almost two thousand years since He ascended up into Heaven. Many generations have come and gone since the Lord told us to do business until I come back. Some have grown weary in well doing, and some have given up. Some have explained it away.

2 Peter 3:4
"Where is the promise of His coming? For since the fathers fell asleep, all things continue as they were from the beginning of creation."

If there ever was an excuse, or a seed of doubt and unbelief, it is this Scripture here explaining the attitude of some people who are on the verge of giving up. It seems that the haters in that generation have something in common with the haters in this generations, they want things to be done right now. If I can't see it, then I won't believe it.

The base principle of this statement is selfishness. It is a lack of patience. It is an excuse to leave our first love and cater to our flesh and speaking foolishly of things we do not comprehend. We don't want to do this by ourselves so we look for like-minded ones to rebel with us. All conspiracies start with the meeting of the minds before they become in one accord on any given subject. In short, it is the story of when two dummies meet.

We can see an example of this in the conspiracy to cover the resurrection of Jesus. The church leaders paid the guards to say that the disciples took the body of Jesus in the middle of the night. They were scared the news of His rising from the dead would be worse than the life He led while alive. [See *Matthew 27:62-65* and *28:11-1*] The lost, the haters, the ones under the guise of the spirit of anti-Christ will always come up with doubt and unbelief in their thoughts and conversations. So when you hear words like, it hasn't changed in 2,000 years or He isn't coming back, you will know that this is nothing new.

> *2 Peter 3:8*
> *But beloved, do not forget this one thing, that with the Lord one day is as a thousand years, and a thousand years are as a day.*

God created time so He lives outside of time. A blink of an eye for God could equal five hundred years for us. We just do not have a concept of time in eternity.

> *2 Peter 3:9*
> *The Lord is not slack concerning His promise, as some count slackness, but is longsuffering toward us, not willing that any should perish but that all should come to repentance.*

God is giving us plenty of time to preach the Gospel to the entire earth and tell them the Good News of His salvation through Jesus Christ our Lord. So if it takes another ten thousand years for Jesus to come back for His Church, then so be it. God wants all people to have the chance to come into His salvation. In the parable of the persistent widow in *Luke 18:8*, Jesus asks this question, *"What kind of faith will He find when He comes back?"*

Then all those virgins arose and trimmed their lamps.

When Jesus does come back, everyone will want to go to Heaven. However it will be too late to make this decision. In all actuality, you made the decision when you first heard about the salvation of the Lord Jesus Christ dying on the cross to pay the penalty for our sins and to purchase a place for us in Heaven. Through all the altar calls that you either put off or dismissed, you actually made a choice to deny Christ. There won't be any time to repent nor time to try to change their ways once that eastern sky lights up with the glory of the Lord riding a horse in the air. If this is you, you need to thank God for second chances or third or fifty or five-hundredth chance. This is one of the reasons He has delayed the coming of His Son to gather the saints from the earth. He knows we are hard-headed at times; He also knows these hard-headed people will get tired of running their heads against the wall of defeat, sickness, disease, failure, bondage and discontent.

And the foolish said to the wise, "Give us some of your oil, for our lamps are going out."

The unprepared know whom to go to when the time of need has come upon them. These are the ones who sit in the background and talk about the ones that are preparing themselves for the service of God. The ones with all the jokes and believes they have plenty of time to get themselves together before Christ's returns. These are the ones who find all the time in the world to play games or participate in the things of the world.

Jesus explains this further in *Luke 12:35-40*. In this passage of Scripture Jesus is teaching His disciples. I want you to notice something, He would teach in parables to the crowds most of the time, but to His disciples, He would give them the Gospel straight and uncut.

He told the disciples to have their waist girded and your lamps burning. To gird yourself is to be ready for action. He is saying to be ready, be full of the spirit, be in contact with the Father, be in constant awareness that you are the dwelling place of Almighty God and be mindful that He lives in us for a reason.

He tells us not to worry about the time, He may come in the second watch or the third watch. This means that He may come in 2016, 2126, or 4026. Jesus will come when God tells Him, "Go get em' Son!" It doesn't matter what time He comes, what matters is that we must have a personal relationship with Him today, that we abide in Him and He abides in us on a daily basis, and sometimes on a moment by moment basis.

He elaborates we should be ready like a slave who waits on his master. He says the servants that are watching and waiting for His return will be blessed. He also promises those who are ready will be able to sit down and eat with the Master, with the Creator of the heavens and earth, the Holy Son of God. We must stay ready and that is an easy thing to do – all you have to do is to submit yourself to be led by the Holy Spirit.

> But the wise answered saying, "No lest there should not be enough for us and you; but go rather to those who sell, and buy for yourselves.
> And while they went to buy, the bridegroom came, and those who were ready went in with him to the wedding; and the door was shut.

When Jesus comes, it will be faster than a blink of the eye; all those who are ready will get to go in with Him. All who are not ready will not get to go with Him – it will be too late!

> Afterward the other virgins came also, saying, "Lord, Lord, open to us!" But he answered and said, 'Assuredly, I say to you, I do not know you."
> Watch therefore, for you know neither the day nor the hour in which the Son of Man is coming.

115

Notes:

Chapter 10
Speaking in Parables *(Part 2)*

The Parable of the Great Supper
In *The Gospel of Luke*, chapter 14, Jesus told a parable about taking the Kingdom of God lightly. In this parable He expresses the importance of listening to the Master and choosing spiritual things instead of worldly things.

> *Then He said to him, "A certain man gave a great supper and invited many, and sent his servant at supper time to say to those who were invited, 'Come, for all things are now ready.'*

In this parable, 'the certain man' is God. The invitation to the great supper is the gift of salvation. The certain man, or God, made the gift of salvation or the great supper, available to every person on the planet. In other words all people are invited to the great supper, or receive the salvation of the Lord.

When Jesus was on the cross and said, *"It is finished!"* He meant the wall of separation was destroyed for those who choose to have God in their lives. The thing that kept us, Gentiles, outside of the covenant has been abolished. It meant the penalty for our sins was now paid in full and the dominion of darkness in our lives had been shattered. It also meant the Jews and Gentiles could become one in the family of God. This is the reason for the celebration of this great supper.

However, everyone will not be excited about the Kingdom of God and will treat it as if it were something trivial or insignificant. Here the Kingdom of God is available to everyone but people have other ideals and interest.

But they all with one accord began to make excuses. The first said to him, 'I have brought a piece of ground, and I must go and see it. I ask you to have me excused.' And another said, 'I have bought five yoke of oxen, and I am going to test them. I ask you to have me excused. I ask that you have me excused.' Still another said, 'I have married a wife, and therefore I cannot come.'

I know this is hard to believe, but everyone does not want the salvation of the Lord. Everyone does not want to be free from demonic possession, oppression, influence, sickness, diseases, bondage to alcohol, bondage to drugs, bondage to sex or bondage to the world. Everyone does not want to be free from a polluted mind with torturous thoughts of the enemy. It is sad but it is true.

Today, we hear a host of excuses on why we shouldn't worship God or honor Jesus Christ as His only begotten Son. People will say that He is not real, or that religion stuff is for weak people. Some call Christianity a religion of escapism, and then there is the always popular, "They're a bunch of fanatics," allegation attached. People make all kinds of excuses for not going to church.

Some will think I've got food in the pantry, gas in the car, my bills are paid, the children are fine and the wife/husband is happy – What more do I need? Just about ninety-nine percent of the time, the foundation of the excuses would be the flesh.

There are seasons when even Christians don't want to go to church. But this is the time when we must put down these thoughts, go against our flesh, and go anyway. Sometimes our flesh just doesn't want to act right and wants to be lazy, but we must put down these thoughts of the flesh because they are not the thoughts of God. The flesh is enmity, hostility, resentment, antagonism, hatred, and animosity, against God.

There have been times in my life when I know there is a church service going on but I want to kick back and 'relax' for a while. Then my spirit begins to stir, telling me that I need to be there. Why? Because God either has a Word for me or He may give me a Word for someone else. We must realize it is not all about us; it is about being in position for God to work through us on behalf of someone else. So if I listen to my flesh and don't go to church, then someone else will not get what he or she needed from the Father. Yes, God can use someone else, but He shouldn't have to go to anyone else because you have proclaimed that you would be His to use in the Kingdom of God. When the Spirit pulls us to go to this particular meeting or that certain service and we don't go, then we are in disobedient to the Spirit.

Even in prison, people use the excuse for not going to an inmate church service because it is full of child molesters and rapist, 'as if it is a worse crime than lying or stealing or killing someone.' Some won't go to particular service because the majority of the people are black people while on the other hand others won't go because the majority is white people. I have heard many excuses on why we shouldn't go to church, and there are no different than the excuses listed in the passage of Scripture above.

The piece of ground, the team of oxen, and the newly married are great things in life. However, the Bible says *'what would it profit for a man to gain the whole world but lose his soul?"* [See *Mark 8:36*] The people's priorities were backwards. These people are an example of worshipping the creation, or giving priority to, things that were made by God instead of God Who made the things. They didn't want to give God the glory for what He has done for them.

Idolatry is very rampant in these United States because most of the people base their lives, or conduct their lives on I, me, or mine. So when we put ourselves above the Lord Jesus Christ, we have placed ourselves in an idolatrous situation.

It is easy to set your mind on physical things instead of spiritual things. The world screams at us for its attention, but as children of God, we must always put God first in every situation. Because as we worship Him for Who He is, He will bless us with the desires of our hearts. It doesn't matter if it is a parcel of land, or livestock, or even a beautiful bride or handsome husband; we must maintain the mindset that God gives us these things, and we should be thankful for them. In our thankfulness, we need to keep out priorities straight.

So that servant came and reported these things to his master. Then the master of the house, being angry, said to his servant, 'Go quickly into the streets and lanes of the city, and bring in here the poor and the maimed, crippled, and the lame and the blind.

You can truly see the nation of Israel in this Scripture. Jesus, the Son of God came to the earth to offer salvation to the Jews first and then to the Gentiles. The Jews turned down the free gift of salvation; this also opened the doors for the Gentiles to receive God's salvation package. The three men who refused the great supper or the great wedding feast are the Jews, salvation comes through the Jews. However salvation for Gentiles actually came through the Jews rejection of Christ Jesus as the Son of the True and Living God. When the Jews rejected God's gracious offer, then the door was opened for the Gentile nations to come into the salvation of God.

And the servant said, 'Master, it is done as you commanded, and still there is room.' Then the master said to the servants, 'Go out into the highways and hedges, and compel them to come in, that my house may be filled. For I say to you that none of those men who were invited shall taste my supper.

We are the ones who were in the streets and lanes of the city. We were the poor and the maimed, and the lame and the blind. We were the ones in the highways and in the hedges. The servants that came and got us are the Evangelists, and the preachers that compelled us to come and receive a new way of life. These men are the ones that are fulfilling the Great Commission in their lives and fulfilling the will of God in ours.

In the 22nd chapter of *The Gospel of Matthew* there is a similar parable named, *The Parable of the Wedding Feast.* It seems that a guest had slipped into a wedding celebration without being clothed in wedding garments. I personally believe that he wasn't clothed with the Holy Spirit. I believe this man didn't have the salvation of God because there wasn't any evidence of a changed life. I believe

120

this man didn't have the joy of the Lord on him. There is another possibility; he may have been a tare in the ceremony. We'll pick up the story at verse 11:

> But when the king came in to see the guest, he saw a man there who did not have on a wedding garment. So he said to him, 'Friend how did you come in here without a wedding garment? And he was speechless. The king said to the servants, 'Bind him hand and foot, take him away, and cast him into outer darkness, there will be weeping and gnashing of teeth.' For many are called and few are chosen.

There are millions of people who believe in almost a million different ways to get into the Kingdom of Heaven. This man is one of them. He tried to sneak into the Kingdom of Heaven. This is very possibly the ones that Jesus tells, *"I never knew you."*

Some people will feel because they had been a deacon in the Church for 50 years, they have earned their way into Heaven. Others feel that because they sat on the fifth pew every Sunday they are saved and will inherit the Kingdom of God. Some feel because they gave to the poor, they have bought the right to enter into the Kingdom of God.

These people do not know that trusting in Christ is the only way to receive salvation. They do not know that obedience to the Word is proof of your conversion. The person that snuck into the wedding feast must have been one that did not know what it takes to receive the free gift of salvation. Or he wasn't a doer of the Word of God. In any event, he was cast out into outer darkness.

Parables of the Minas

In *Luke 19*, we find an interesting parable based on the Kingdom of God.

> Now as they heard these things, He spoke another parable, because He was near Jerusalem and because they thought the Kingdom of God would appear immediately.

Jesus had just left Zacchaeus' house and His face was set for Jerusalem. He knew His time was growing short but He still had some teaching to do with His disciples on the Kingdom of God. They were still not sure what the true Kingdom meant. At this time, they thought that the Kingdom of God was a physical kingdom. All through history, the kingdoms were physical kingdoms with a physical king sitting on the throne ruling his kingdom. It is no doubt they knew about King Saul, David, Solomon, and Josiah and all the rest the kings of Judah and Israel that were written in the Chronicles of the Kings. We must remember the disciples had not received the Holy Spirit as of yet, so they also couldn't discern what the Kingdom of God truly meant. So the disciples were under the impression that Jesus was going to Jerusalem to initiate the Kingdom of God in a physical sense.

So Jesus began by telling them a story that depicts the spiritual truth.

Therefore He said: "A certain nobleman went into a far country to receive for himself a kingdom and to return.

Jesus is talking about Himself as the nobleman in this parable. There's no one nobler the Jesus the Anointed One, the Son of the Most High God. In all actuality, He came from Heaven to earth, but in this parable, he is here on earth. The far country is Heaven. After He receives His Kingdom, He will return.

Revelation 11:15
Then the seventh angel sounded: And there were loud voices in heaven, saying, "The Kingdoms of this world have become the kingdoms of our Lord and of His Christ, and He shall reign forever and ever!"

In the Kingdom of God what the disciples were expecting will not happen until just before the seventh angel sounds his trumpet. This is the physical Kingdom of God the disciples were looking for. After this happens, God directs His punishment on unbelievers and the wages of our decisions will be rendered.

The Kingdom of God was ordained at that time, as a spiritual Kingdom. It was the Holy Spirit coming to dwell in the hearts of men in order to carry out the will of God for humanity.

In *Luke 17: 20-21*, Jesus tells the Pharisees that the Kingdom will not come with a lot of pomp, celebrations, and fireworks as they were expecting. They were looking into the natural realm for a spiritual revolution. This is like shopping for pipe wrenches in a fast food restaurant.

Jesus went on to say that the Kingdom of God will be within you. He was talking about the new birth, the new creation, or the born-again experience. He was talking about God fulfilling the prophecy of creating in men a clean heart; one not made of flesh or the circumcision of the heart. Jesus was talking about the Holy Spirit, the Spirit of God, dwelling in the hearts of men. So Jesus set the stage for the entrance of the Kingdom of God.

*So he called ten of his servants, delivered to them ten minas,
and said to them, 'Do business till I come.'*

A mina is equivalent to about three month's salary. Each of these servants received one mina and was told to do business until He came back. Kingdom business is evangelizing and reconciling the chosen to Jesus Christ.

The mina in this parable represents abilities or gifts or talents God blesses us with for use as spiritual tools as the Holy Spirit wills. The purpose of these abilities and gifts are for us, the Church, to use as tools for the advancement of the kingdom of God. The minas in this parable and the parable of the talents in *Matthew 25* have the same theme and as stewards of the Word of God, we should heed the message in these parables.

This message from Jesus is not to outsiders; He is talking to the Church, the body of Christ. He may have been talking to the disciples, but the assignment for the disciples is to preach the Gospel to the ends of the earth. This started with Jerusalem, then to Judea, to

Samaria and to the ends of the earth. This lesson is for the disciples then and the Body of Christ now.

Jesus has given us spiritual gifts such as a word of wisdom, word of knowledge, the gift of faith, gifts of healings, working of miracles, prophesy, discerning of spirits, tongues, and interpretation of tongues which are listed in *1 Corinthians 12-14*. In *Ephesians 4*, the Bible tells us that *He gave gifts to men* such as Apostles, Prophets, Evangelists, Pastors and Teachers for the equipping of the saints and for the work of the ministry, for the building up of the body of Christ. The gift He gave was Himself.

> *But the citizens hated him, and sent a delegation after him, saying, "We will not have this man to reign over us.*

Jesus told His disciples the world hated Him without a cause. [See *John 15:25*] Why? Most people do not want change unless it is threatening their life, or the life of a loved one. But until then, let's eat, drink, and be merry and do whatever feels good.

But to those who are sick and tired of being captive to sin and the lure has lost its luster, there is hope. That hope is in Jesus Christ. A person cannot come to Christ unless he or she is sick and tired of the old life. They have to be sick and tired of being used by the enemy, tired of being pimped and prostituted in the bowls of sin, tired of being defeated, and distrusted, where confusion, mystification, perplexity, and bafflement is the constant struggle called life.

Those who believe in Jesus as the Son of God have the ability to break the mold of the old lifestyle and be regenerated in a new life style, a holy life style, a life style that is pleasing to God.

People hated Jesus because He called sin – sin. He didn't sugar coat it, nor did He did pacify it. When people were outside the will of God, He told them plainly they were outside the boundaries of Kingdom of God. He didn't care who they were or what position they held. If you were wrong, you were wrong.

The mission of Jesus was to straighten the path for mankind and to light up the road to Heaven so that people could follow the Light from the world into eternal life. The world had gotten off-track during the past 4,000 years and had gotten comfortable in the spiritual quagmire they were living in. Jesus came and reminded them of what God expected.

Habits are hard to break, and the religious sects in those days were comfortable in their false sense of holiness and righteousness. Their sanctification had become a farce because they separated themselves unto themselves. So Jesus upset their religious and their personal order in worshipping God.

There isn't any difference today in these religious characteristics and the days when our Lord walked the face off the earth. Humanity either loves Him or hates Him. As the delegation sent word to him in the parable, folks today also show they don't want Him to be king in their lives. This is made evident in the lifestyle of each and every individual. It is shown in our speech, our activities, and the desires of our hearts. As stated before, when a person lives unto himself, or in the flesh, then he or she finds themselves on the other side of the fence, or in opposition of what Jesus stands for. The sins of yesterday are still sins today.

> *And so it was that when he returned, having received the kingdom, he then commanded these servants, to whom he had given the money, to be called to him, that he might know how much every man had gained by trading.*

When the king came back, it was accountability time. The king holds his subjects, his servants accountable for the money, the talents, and the gifts he had given to them. He will be asking "What did you do with the free gift of salvation that I purchased with my own blood?"

> *Then came the first, saying, 'Master, your mina has earned ten minas.' And he said to him, "Well done good servant; because you were faithful in a very little, have authority over ten cities.'*

The first servant came to the king and presented his work to him.

125

He didn't just double the money; he made it ten times over. The king was very pleased with him, and said, *"Well done thy good and faithful servant. You have been faithful over a small business, I will multiply you and give you charge over ten cities."*

And the second came, saying, 'Master, your mina has earned five minas.' And he said to him, "You also be over five cities.

When Jesus comes back, He will hold the Church accountable for the gifts He gave to accomplish the task He gave us to do. For instance, if Jesus gave me the gifts of healings and I used that gift for His glory, then I would hear the same thing He told His servants. *"Well done thy good and faithful servant. You were faithful over a few things, I will make you ruler over many things. Enter into the joy of your Lord."* [See *Matthew 25:21*] It doesn't matter if it was the gifts or healing or preaching the Gospel or sweeping the church house floor. It doesn't matter if you drive the church bus or if you are the treasurer of the church. He gave us all gifts to use for the edifying of the body of Christ. When we use what He gave us, then we will be called highly favored, we will no longer be called servants but friends. [See *John 15:15*]

Just as every man is given a measure of faith, we are also given a talent. We must work the talent He gave us; we must perfect this gift by using it for the glory of His Kingdom. It takes practice to perfect the gifts that He gives to us. Like the first man, we can multiply what He has given to us at least ten-fold.

This means if He gives you twenty men to teach the Word of God to. Then you teach His word faithfully and truthfully for as long as it takes. If you are faithful with these twenty men, God will add the increase and you will then find yourself teaching twenty thousand men. The Bible tells us that it is the Holy Spirit that draws men unto the Kingdom of God. Since this is true, then we must not offend the Holy Spirit by neglecting to use the gifts and the talents that were given to us to expand the Kingdom of God.

Then another came saying, 'Master, here is your mina, which I have kept put away in a handkerchief. For I feared you, because you are an austere man. You collect what you did not deposit, and reap what you did not sow.'

If there was ever a man in trouble, this is the man. This man actually had a hatred for his master. Whatever you fear, you will hate. This man didn't do anything with the money he had received. He didn't do any trading to increase the money nor did he put it in a bank to draw interest. He just sat on it, buried it and went about being useless. He probably sat around talking about what's wrong with this and what's wrong with that. I believe he was one that was never satisfied with anything that went on in his life. This man was a malcontent in every area of life. So because the servant was not in one mind and one accord with his master, the master called him a wicked and lazy servant. [See *Matthew 25:26*] When the servant says, I know that you are a very strict God. It would be like icing on the cake.

Today, this parallels a person who had the twenty men to teach the principles of the Kingdom of God. But this man didn't teach the basic principles of the Kingdom. He buried the truth of God's Word and kicked back.

There are too many preachers and teachers who believe it is their obligation to talk about other servants of God. Why would one do such a thing? There are ministries that devote their time and money talking about other ministers. He missed it here or he missed it there. He is taking this Scripture out of context or that ideal out of context. What they are doing right and what they are doing wrong. Some folks call it, 'keeping the cheat off!" This is a person that talks about another in order shift focus and attention from of their own personal shortcomings to others. If one was to get people to concentrate on someone else's sin then they won't be concentrating on his. God calls this being a busy body. When we spend our time looking at what other ministers are doing, then we have obviously taken our eyes off of God. God will judge His ministers with what He gave them.

These men will either abuse the gift God gave them or they will not use it. Either way, there would not be any expansion of the Kingdom of God. There wouldn't be any growth in the Church, or the individuals in the Church. They would go to church once a week in a stale condition and leave in the same stale condition they came in. There is no deliverance from anything in these types of churches. They are just as bound as the lost people in the world are and they are only churches in name only.

In this parable the servant knew that the king was an austere man. An austere man is one that is severe, stern, or strict in his ways.

And he said to him, 'Out of your own mouth I will judge you, you wicked servant. You knew that I was an austere man, collecting what I did not deposit and reaping what I did not sow. Why then did you not put my money in the bank, that at my coming I might have collected it with interest?"

He knew that the master was stern in his ways. He is a shrewd businessman and making a profit was his top priority. The master didn't care how he made his money, because it says he collected what he did not deposit. That really sounds like robbery. He collected, gained in things that he was not a part of. I imagine that would be like someone starting a business and after the business was up and running, another man would commandeer the business for himself. I believe this was the mental picture the servant had of his master.

When we come to the Judgment Seat of Christ on Judgment Day with the abilities that He gave us unused, uncultured, unaccomplished, incomplete, non-proficient, unfinished, and uncultivated; He will ask us why didn't we use the gifts He gave us for His Kingdom? Why didn't we go to the lost and offer tell them of the gift of salvation? Why didn't you use the teaching gift that I gave you in order to teach My Word so they can understand? Why didn't you lay hands on the sick so they can recover? Why didn't you cast out demons that were binding people in mental hospitals and on street corners? Why didn't you go and visit those in prison? Why didn't you give a cup of cold water to one of these little ones? Why didn't you comfort those who were tormented and confused? Why didn't you explain the Good News of who we are in Christ Jesus?

For those who were operating in a spirit of error, He would probably go on to say, "Why did you teach things that are not in My covenant? Why did you take the money and use it on yourself instead of feeding My lambs, My sheep, and tending to the needs of My children? Why did you treat My holiness as a common thing? Why did you lie on My son? Why did you teach that I was no longer performing miracles and caused unbelief to spread throughout the land? Why did you lead them astray?"

> *And he said to those who stood by, take the mina from him, and give it to him who has ten minas.' But they said to him, Master, he has ten minas.'*

This is a prime example of the rewards the Believer will receive in Heaven, which are based on his works through the Holy Spirit while on the earth. *Ephesians 2:10* says we are created for good works and God will reward those who are obedient to His Word. For those who fulfill His purpose on the earth will hear these wonderful Words that could melt the heart away.

> *For I say to you, that to everyone who has will be given; and from him who does not have, even what he has will be taken away from him.*

If we hold on to material things, then we haven't died to ourselves. If we hold material things in such high esteem and won't allow Christ to have His way in our life, then what we have will be taken away from us. Whatever keeps us from the life of Christ is spiritually killing us and if we chose things of the world, then He is not our Lord and Savior. You have chosen or created another.

The rule of God demands that we are fearless in spreading the truth of the Gospel. There will even be a little risk taking involved. That is one reason why it is so important to be led by His Spirit. We have a lot of opposition in the world. There is our common enemy Satan, and countless people who do not have the Spirit of God who will try to discourage you and if possible, stop you from fulfilling your purpose. The Apostle John said 2,000 years ago that there are many anti-Christ's in the world. Anti-Christ simply means people that are in opposition, conflict, hostility, contention, and in strife, against God's Christ.

Christians who are carrying out the will of God will run into some downright scary people at times. There are some people who feel threatened by the Good News of salvation. And then, there are some people that just downright hate the Good News of salvation. Finally there are the ones who receive the free gift of salvation with joy and their lives are changed. It is a war, a spiritual war, but God has shown the true believer the outcome, we win!

The brothers and sisters that are fearlessly carrying out the Word of God without any apprehension of death have this promise; those who lose their life for My sake will find life, eternal life. Not only eternal life, but the rewards of Heaven, the rewards of God in eternal life are too big, too much, too high to even imagine. To tell the truth, our feeble minds cannot grasp all the goodness that our King has for us after we die and join Him in eternal life.

But bring here those enemies of mine, who did not want me to reign over them, and slay them before me.

For those who do not find themselves at the Judgment Seat of Christ but in front of God at the Great White Throne Judgment will be in serious trouble for the rest of their eternal lives. This is called the second death.

Revelation 21:8
But the cowardly, unbelieving, abominable, murderers, sexually immoral, sorcerers, idolaters, and all liars shall have their part in the lake of fire and brimstone, which is the second death.

The cowardly are those who allow the world to manipulate, or scare them into not fulfilling the will of God in their lives. Those who are too scared to preach the Gospel for whatever reason they

130

conjure up. Jesus tells us *not to fear man who can only kill you, but fear God Who can kill you and cast you in hell.* [See *Luke 12:4-5*]

The unbelieving are those who are actually calling God a liar. They don't believe Him and they don't believe His Word. In any event, they chose the second death for themselves.

The abominable are the things that God hates as we discussed in an earlier chapter. Those with murderous hearts, hatred and ill will for others also will take their part in the second death. Those who are sexually immoral and selling themselves for sexual purposes or selling their sexuality for people to buy cars, hamburgers, jet skis, cupcakes, dining room tables and a host of other products will have their part in the second death. Those who sleep around and use their victims as sexual trophies will have their part in the second death.

Those who practice sorcery, which includes astrology, tarot cards, incantations, spells and drugs that alter the mind, will have their part in the second death. Those who conjure demonic spirits, and play Dungeons and Dragons, (practice) Ouija and other board games that entail magic, demons, and charms will take their part in the second death.

Those who worship anyone or anything else but God are idolaters. All those who do not accept Jesus Christ as the Son of God are practicing idolatry. All those who believe they can have God without Christ have missed it and will take their part in the second death.

All those who misrepresent the truth will also have their part in the second death. Whether they are white lies, bold face lies, or little itsy bitsy lies. Lies are lies when they deviate from the truth. All of those who practice these traits will find themselves in front of God and will be sentenced without the possibility of parole to the second death, which is the lake that burns with fire and brimstone.

It is a very serious thing for a Christian to be lazy and not use the talents, or gifts that God gives us to help our fellow man in this world come to the knowledge of Christ.

The Parable of the Vineyard
This parable is preceded by the parable of the minas.

Matthew 20:1-2
For the kingdom of heaven is like a landowner who went
out early in the morning to hire laborers for his vineyard. Now
when he had agreed with the laborers for a denarius a day, he
sent them into his vineyard.

This parable stretches through time. The landowner is God
and the laborers are Israel. God created Israel from the Patriarch
Abraham;this was the first step in God's salvation plan. He created
a nation, blessed them and called them His children. He made a
covenant with Israel with the promise of a Savior coming from the
bloodline of Abraham to reconcile the nations back to God. Even
though Israel was the chosen people, God had planned to include
Gentiles at the proper time. Abraham, Isaac and Jacob, the Patri-
archs of Israel are the early morning workers.

v 3-4
And he went out about the third hour and saw others stand-
ing idle in the market place, and said to them, you also go into
the vineyard, and whatever is right I will give you. So they went.

The third hour is about nine am but in reality, it's about four
hundred years later. God told Abraham his offspring would spent
four hundred years in captivity in a foreign land and they will be
afflicted. [See *Genesis 15:12*] About seventy-five descendants went
into Egypt and the nation grew to approximately 3 to 6 million by
the time Moses was born. God raised up Moses and Aaron for the
task of freeing Israel from Egypt and their host of gods. Egypt represents the world's system which includes idolatry.

vs 5-7
Again he went out about the sixth and the ninth hour, and
did likewise. And about the eleventh hour he went out and
found others standing idle, and said to them, "Why have you
been standing here idle all day? They said to him, "because no

one hired us.' He said to them, 'You go into my vineyard, and whatever is right you will receive.

The sixth hour is twelve noon and the ninth hour is 3 pm. Again, several hundreds of years have passed from the early morning to 3 pm in universal time, or the world's time clock. When it was close to the end of the day, God was still hiring people to work in his vineyard.

During the sixth hour God was preparing His Kingdom through King David, King Solomon and others. During the ninth hour, the time of prophesies, God used His Prophets to convey what "Thus said the Lord" to His children. Warning the faithless of their waywardness and promising the faithful great and wonderful things.

The eleventh hour is the age of Christianity.

> *v 8*
> *So when evening had come, the owner of the vineyard said to his steward, "Call the laborers and give them their wages, beginning with the last to the first.*

At the end of the day, God called all the workers to give them their wages. However, He started with the eleventh hour workers and gave them a denarius.

> *vs 9-10*
> *And when those who were hired at the eleventh hour, they each received a denarius. But when the first came, they supposed that they would receive more, and they likewise received each a denarius.*

When the early workers, (Israel) saw the late workers (Christians) each received a denarius, they thought they would receive more money than agreed upon.

> *vs 11-12*
> *And when they had received it, they complained against the*

landowner, saying, these last men have worked only one hour, and you have made them equal to us who have borne the burden and the heat of the day.

The early workers were and will be offended because the late workers were equally paid. They were and will be upset because they bore the burden of the heat or the burden of keeping the law for approximately three thousand years, but failed to do so. When Jesus died on the cross, the Gentiles were made equal with the Jews because salvation was now an open offer to the entire world.

> *Romans 11:18*
> *For if the first fruit is holy, the lump is also holy; and if the root is holy, so are the branches. And if some of the branches were broken off, and you, being a wild olive tree, were grafted in among them, and with them became a partaker of the root and fatness of the olive tree, do not boast against the branches. But if you do boast, remember that you do not support the root, but the root supports you.*

Abraham is the root of Israel; he was holy, faithful and obedient to the Word of God. He is the father of Israel as well as the patriarch because God made the nation from his loins. Remember, whosoever blesses Abraham will be blessed and whoever curses Abraham shall be cursed. The promise of God is for the entire world could be blessed through Abraham which was step one in God's process of reconciliation. The Jews were first to have a covenant with God, then the Gentiles.

When Jesus was rejected by the Jews, their branch was broken off the vine and Gentiles were grafted into the olive tree, or the Kingdom of God. Israel's rejection became the Gentile's acceptance because those who believe became partakers of the rich and spiritual nourishment that comes from the vine/olive tree.

> *Romans 11:19-21*
> *You will say then, "Branches were broken off that I might be*

grafted in." Well said, because of unbelief they were broken off, and you stand by faith. Do not be haughty, but fear. For if God did not spare the natural branches, He may not spare you either.

We are saved by grace and we cannot boast in our abilities and we certainly cannot boast against Israel. We were on the outside looking in and God blessed us to be His children. We cannot disrespect Israel because they were broken off, but we are thankful that God has imparted Himself to us, cleansed us from our sins, and gave us a new nature to walk in the covenant He cut with us. This is just one of the reasons we live a life of humility, meekness, love as we walk by faith and not by sight. Israel lost her way through the years and because of that, Gentiles have the opportunity to become children of God.

> *vs 13-15*
> *But he answered one of them and said, 'Friend, I am doing you no wrong. Did you not agree with me for a denarius? Take what is yours and go your way. I wish to give to this last man the same as you. Is it not lawful for me to do what I wish with my own things? Or is your eye evil because I am good?*

God is good and He has been good to us even when we don't deserve it, even when we act out, even when we're lazy, even when we miss the mark. Whatever gifts He has given us, we should be appreciative for the blessings he has bestowed upon us. If we have a job, then we should be happy with our job. If He has given us a spouse, then be happy with your spouse He has given you. If you are walking in good health, you need to praise God and thank Him for your good health, your transportation, and even your bank account.

I believe we are in the eleventh hour of God's universal clock – if not eleven then ten thirty. In any event, we are close to the return of Jesus the Messiah, Jesus the Christ. It is God's will that every person on the planet has to have the opportunity to hear of Christ's salvation plan. It doesn't matter if the last person to hear the Gospel is on the African savannah, the South American rain forest, the frozen tundra of Antarctica, up North, down South, in the East, or out West. Jesus will not come back for His Church until every human has a chance to say, "Save me Lord." When the last Gentile crosses over from heathen to Christianity, then Jesus will come. No one knows the date or time He will return but He gave clues according to seasons, the attitude of people, and current events.

> *v 16*
> *So the last will be first and the first last. For many are called but few are chosen.*

Adam and Eve were the first people in covenant with God, and then years later, the Nation of Israel was called into covenant with Him. They would live righteously for forty or so years and then rebel for twenty years until God would send a foreign army to punish them. We are in a new covenant which is a much better covenant because God has made Himself available to have a personal relationship with His children, who abides in us and we in Him,

God has called many people into His service, but only the faithful and obedient are chosen.

Notes:

Chapter 11

Speaking in Parables *(Part 3)*

The Parable of the Rich Fool

Luke 12:13-21

Then one from the crowd said to Him, "Teacher, tell my brother to divide the inheritance with me."

But He said to him, Man, who made Me a judge or an arbitrator over You? And He said to them, "Take heed and beware of covetousness. For one's life does not consist in the abundance of things he possesses."

Then He spoke a parable to them saying, "The ground of a certain rich man yielded plentifully, and he thought within himself, saying "What shall I do, since I have I have no room to store my crops? So he said I will do this: I will pull down my barn and build greater, and there I will store all my crops and my goods. And I will say to my soul, Soul, you have many goods laid up for many years; take your ease; eat drink and be merry." But God said to him; Fool! This night your soul will be required of you; then whose things will they be which you have provided?

So is he who lays up treasure for himself, and is not rich toward God."

There is nothing wrong with being rich in goods or money if your heart is right with God. There will be people who were rich in this life in Heaven because they did not rely on their riches for salvation. The question is, what did they do with the money? Did they hoard the money for themselves? Did they stay up night and day trying to make money and thus push the will of God away? I want you to notice something in the speech pattern of the rich fool.

What shall I do?
¬I have no room for my crops
I will do this
I will pull down my barns and build greater barns
I will store all my goods
I will say to my soul

There is no room for selfishness in the Kingdom of God. It is not about me, it is about faith in action. It is about loving and sharing with those who are lost and less fortunate. Just as Jesus fed the five thousand and then the four thousand, we should use our money to help others. We should not focus on ourselves but in the needs of others. When we do this unselfishly, then we are rich toward God.

Now when I hear a series of I's, I think about Lucifer's thoughts before he was demoted to Satan the Dragon. How he wanted to set his throne above God's throne.

God calls the rich man a fool and said that his soul was required that night! Then he posed a question, when you die, who will get all the material things you accumulated? Where will your money go? We can spend our lives gathering all the material items we want, but in the end, all the work we've done will go to someone else.

There are preachers here in the United States of America that has accumulated tons of money and bought or built enormous castle like mansions. Some have a fleet of jets and their own personal airport. But when these preachers and teachers pass away, all their possessions will go to someone else. It is best to share while we are alive than to share after we die.

The Parable of the Persistent Widow
Luke 19:1-8
Then He spoke a parable to them, that men always ought to pray and not lose heart, saying: "There was in a certain city a judge who did not fear God nor regard man. Now there was

a widow in that city; and she came to him saying, 'Get justice for me from my adversary.' And he would not for a while; but afterward he said within himself, though I do not fear God nor regard man, yet because this widow troubles me I will avenge her, lest by her continual coming she weary me.

Then the Lord said, "Hear what the unjust judge said. And shall God not avenge His own elect who cry out day and night to Him, though He bears long with them? I tell you that He will avenge them speedily. Nevertheless, when the Son of Man comes, will He really find faith on the earth?

This parable pertains to having a 'never give up' attitude in your prayer life. Jesus tells us that we are to pray, that we ought to pray and never lose heart or never give up. Sometimes it takes a while to get a prayer answered but God will answer it. Remember it took twenty-five years before Abraham got his son. It took thirteen years before Joseph was released from prison and elevated to the palace as the vice-president of Egypt.

If an old lady can wear down a judge that does not fear God nor have any regard for man, won't God take care of His own? Jesus says that He will never leave us nor forsake us.

Matthew 7:7
Ask, and it will be given to you; seek, and you will find; knock, and it will be opened to you.

Jesus tells us to *ask and it will be given to us* – point blank! He tells us to *seek and we will find* – point blank! He tells us to *knock and the door will be open to us* - again point blank. Jesus says when we do these things, we will get results. He did not say we might get results or maybe we will get results or if it is a good day, we will get results – He said it will be given to you. He said you will find what you are looking for and the door will be opened to you. If you have the faith to believe that God is not a liar and will give to you what you ask – then you shall receive an answer to your prayer.

James 5:14-15a

Is anyone among you sick? Let him call the elders of the church, and let them pray over him, anointing him with oil in the name of the Lord. And the prayer of faith will save the sick, and the Lord will raise him up...

Prayer is communication with God. If your prayer life is not where it needs to be for whatever reason, then call on the elders of the Church, or someone with a prayer life to pray over the person. When we pray we should anoint them with oil, or lay hands on the person seeking an answer from the Lord, in the Name of the Lord Jesus.

Elders in the Church should be powerful men and women of faith. They should be *strong in the Lord and the power of His might.* Elders should have a track record of spiritual strength because of the many battles, circumstances, and situations they have come through. Elders in the Church should be mature in the faith, not age, but faith. Not wavering, not in and out, not doubtful but weather-worn prayer warriors who know their God and know they will receive an answer from the Lord.

The prayer of faith knows that God is just and faithful to answer your prayer according to the Scriptures. If Jesus healed the Centurion because of his faith, He will surely heal anyone who has the faith that He is willing to heal you according to the Scriptures.   The prayer of faith will heal the sick and it will be the Lord that raises him up.

The Parable of the Wheat and Tares

Matthew 13:24-30

Another parable He put forth to them, saying: The King-dom of Heaven is like a man who sowed good seed in his field; but while men slept, his enemy came and sowed tares among the wheat and went his way. But when the grain had sprouted and produced a crop, then the tares also appeared. So the ser-vants of the owner came and said to him, 'Sir, did you not sow good seed in tour field? How then does it have tares? He said to them, 'An enemy has done this.' The servant said to him,

140

'Do you want us then to go and gather them up?' But he said, 'No. lest you gather up the tares you also uproot the wheat with them. Let them both grow together until the end of the harvest, and at the time of harvest I will say to the reapers, "First gather together the tares and bind them in bundles to burn them, but gather the wheat into my barn.

Jesus is the One who sows the good seed, the news of His salvation. The field is the world and the good seeds are the sons of the Kingdom, but the tares are the sons of the wicked one. The enemy who sowed them is the devil, the harvest is the end of the age, and the reapers are angels.

It is Jesus that came to earth to offer us salvation. It is Jesus the Christ that sows goodness in the hearts of men. Those who accepted Christ our Lord are considered the wheat in this parable and the tares are the antichrist. Saved people and antichrist will co-exist until Jesus comes for His Church. Until then, the Church has to be the light and share with the lost the Good News of the Gospel of Christ. Jesus tells us that we are in the world but not of the world. So we as the Body of Christ should not be influenced by the world but to be an influence to the world. We are a reflection of the light of Jesus Christ and we operate from a position of strength *because greater is He that is in us then he that in the world.* So until the day when Jesus sends his angels to reap the earth [See *Revelation 14:14-16*], we will live around the sons of Satan.

The devil sows tares in the world and he also sows tares in the Church. It has been said that tares and wheat appear to be identical. The purpose for the seed sown by Satan is to enslave the world in sin and disrupt the flow of the Church or any move of God for that matter. They are designed to speak words of doubt, unbelief, and cause disruption, disturbance, commotion, interference, disorder, distraction, and downright trouble in the midst of the Church and in the world.

The Boston marathon bombing, the Oklahoma City bombing, 911, the school shootings across the planet, parents killing their children and children killing their parents, rapes, robbers, sex ped-

141

dlers, extortions, the wars overseas and the killing of people around the world, (for whatever reason) are all attributed to tares, and the father of tares is the devil, the king of the kingdom of darkness.

So we, the Body of Christ must keep ourselves from the world where the tares are king. We are not to be influenced by them. We are to influence the world as Jesus did and be a light to all nations. Since we have the greater One in us, we will be able to bring light to this dark and dying world just as our Master did. And just as in the days of Jesus upon this earth, some will accept it, and some will not. There will be some that say they do but they really don't. And there will be some who will go through any means necessary, to stop the move of God on this earth.

There are some people that go to church who are not genuinely saved because they are still operating in the same lifestyle before they joined the church. *"They honor Me with their lips but their hearts are far from Me."* Like the first seed in the parable of the sower, they do not particularly care for the Word of God and generally become a distraction in the Church.

Notes:

Chapter 12

Producing Good Fruit

Bearing Fruit

Luke 3:8

Then He said to the multitude that came out to be baptized by him, "Brood of vipers! Who warned you to flee from the wrath to come? Therefore bear fruit worthy of repentance...

Bearing fruit worthy of repentance is basically changing your life from doing evil deeds to righteous deeds. After John the Baptist made his remark about men and women as sons of snakes, they asked what they should do. John replied, *"He who has two tunics, let him give to him who has none; and he who has food, let him do likewise."*

To the tax collectors he told them, *"Collect no more than what is appointed for you."*

He said to the soldiers, *"Do not intimidate anyone or accuse someone falsely, and be content with your wages."*

Apparently, the Jewish tax collectors the Roman government appointed to collect taxes were over charging the citizens. If a citizen of Jerusalem owed a copper coin, the tax collectors would charge two or three copper coins and pocket the extra coins for themselves.

Some of the soldiers acted more like street gangs or the mafia than the protectors of the city. They extorted, they falsely accused citizens, they had them jailed or imprisoned, some were raped and some were killed. John told them to be content, or be happy with your wages.

There are two kinds of fruit mentioned in the Bible – good fruit and bad fruit. It is impossible for a good tree to bear bad fruit just as it is impossible for a bad tree to bear good fruit. This means you cannot live an evil life and be good to people or even bless people. Those who don't know Jesus can't help but produce bad fruit or evil deeds.

Bearing good fruit is basically treating others kindly. It is being nice, caring sympathetic, compassionate, and courteous to others; bearing good fruit loves others in an innocent and wholesome way. Bearing fruit is a righteous way of life, it loves one another, living in peace with your neighbors, having joy in your life and spreading it to others, it is being gentle with people – even people who are hard to be gentle with; it is a life of self-control and a life in communion with The Holy Ghost.

James 2:14-16
What does it profit, my brethren, if someone says he has faith but does not have works? Can faith save him? If a brother or sister is naked and destitute of daily food, and one of you says to them, "Depart in peace, be warned and filled," but you do not give them the things which are needed for the body, what does it profit.

This is a sad representative of a Christian. Faith is verb, an action word and when we fail to take action in any situation where we can make a difference in someone's life, then our faith is worthless. When we show our works by our faith, then we are bearing good fruit.

Bearing good fruit and faith goes hand in hand. You cannot bear good fruit without faith and you must have faith to bear good fruit. God gives to each person a measure of faith. When we as the Body of Christ use our faith to help others we are bearing good fruit.

vs 17-18
Thus also faith by itself, if it does not have works, is dead. But someone will say, "You have faith, and I have works." Show me your faith without works and I will show you faith by my works.

Faith without works is dead. You can have all the faith in the world, but if you don't use it - you are useless. It takes faith to believe in God, Jesus and the Holy Spirit. It takes faith just to live in the

144

Kingdom of God for without it, you cannot be saved and you will not be able to enter into the Kingdom of God.

There are several people in the Bible who demonstrated their faith throughout the Bible. Abraham, the father of faith was told that he would be the father of many nations and Abraham believed Him and twenty-five years later he was a proud papa. Rahab the prostitute used her faith with her works when she directed the scouts of Israel a different way to avoid detection.

God told Noah to build an ark for God was sending a flood, and Noah used his faith in God's Word and built the ark. David believed and therefore proclaimed his victory over Goliath before he killed him. David told Goliath the Lord will deliver him into his hands. Then he proceeded to kill him.

When Jesus told the man with the withered hand to stretch it out, by faith the man stretched it out and it became whole. When the four men brought their friend to Jesus and had to tear a hole in the roof – their faith was working with their actions.

In *Acts 5*, the faith of the people was so strong; they complimented it by their works and laid the sick on couches in the streets so that the shadow of Peter would fall on them. Later, a multitude from the surrounding areas of Jerusalem came to the Apostles bringing the sick, the lame and those who were tormented by unclean spirits, and they were all healed.

All of these people, these heroes of the Bible saw the fruits of their labor. Their faith was demonstrated by works and good fruit was the outcome.

Matthew 7:16-20
You will know them by their fruits. "Do men gather grapes from thorn bushes or figs from thistles? Even so, every good tree bears good fruit, but a bad tree bears bad fruit. A good tree cannot bear bad fruit nor can a bad tree bear good fruit. Every tree that does not bear good fruit is cut down and thrown into the fire. Therefore, by their fruits you will know them. (False prophets)

People are either good or bad. Good people cannot bear bad fruit because fruit comes from the core of an individual, or the heart. Bad people cannot bear good fruit because their heart is lustful and full of carnality. Even when a person bears bad fruit but does good things it is truly an imposter and his works are a farce, a sham, or a travesty. For instance, Bill Cosby was a philanthropist, he gave millions to different charities, schools and colleges, and sponsored numerous causes, but in the end, he will be known as a great comedian who had the heart of an accused rapist. The Bible says *your sins will find you out.*

Jesus was not only talking about regular people here; He was also talking about false preachers/teachers/prophets. False prophets say they are men of God, however; their hearts and lifestyles are different from their confession. For instance, there is a woman who pastors 'The Gospel from the Stripper's Pole'. It is said she is an ex-stripper that was saved by grace. However, she teaches with most of her breast (nipples) exposed to her congregation and the camcorders. This is bad fruit. There is an African minister who forbids his female congregation to wear underwear. This is bad fruit. There is a pastor in the southern United States that mounts another male in front of the altar in the church. This is bad fruit. There's a female choir director in Alabama that twerks when she directs the choir. Twerking is the bouncing booty dance that is seen in clubs and videos. This is bad fruit. There are some pastors who have sex with women of the church to cleanse them from their sins. This is bad fruit. These are a few examples of people saying they are bearing good fruit but in all reality, their fruit is bad, demonic and satanic.

Romans 1:13
Now I do not want you to be unaware brethren that I often planned to come to you (but was hindered until now), that I might have some fruit among you also, just as among the other Gentiles.

Jesus is the best example of bearing good fruit. He came to earth to give us life; he taught us the way to live and how to worship God. The Apostle Paul also was a bearer of good fruit. After he found his real purpose in life while on the road to Damascus, he began 'being about his Father's business'. He preached and taught and planted churches wherever he went. He demonstrated the wisdom and the power of God when he came across circumstances and situations he acted accordingly. Like Jesus, he healed the sick, he raised the dead, he was bitten by a poisonous snake without any indication he was bitten at all, and he did not deviate from the Word of God.

In Paul's letter to Rome, he thanked God for their faith in Jesus Christ. He wanted to go to Rome to impart a spiritual gift that will continue to help them grow in the knowledge and wisdom of Christ. He was looking to see the fruit for himself – the evidence of salvation.

But now Christ is risen from the dead, and has become the first fruits if those who have fallen asleep. For since by man came death, by Man also came the resurrection of the dead. For as in Adam all die, even so in Christ all shall be made alive. But each one in his own order; Christ the first fruits, afterward those who are in Christ.

When Christ arose from the grave, He became the very first fruit of many men and women that would appreciate Christ who died for their sins. We the body of Christ are good fruit, we have been chosen from the foundation of the world to do good things. The Bible tells us that we are God's workmanship, created in Christ Jesus for good works, (or for good fruit), which God prepared beforehand that we should walk in them.

We must remember that fruit is grown – it is not just given. We take what talent or gift that God gives us and we cultivate it, nurture it, develop it, support it, and improve it. When we add faith with works, then our fruit will be great.

Notes:

Chapter 13

The Vine and the Branches

The Vine

Jesus explains the importance of abiding in the Word in this parable of the vine. It reveals truths of the importance of our life in Christ Jesus. As with all Scripture, this teaching of the vine provides us with accurate information in our relationship as Christians in Christ.

I am the true vine, and My Father is the Vinedresser.

Jesus is the true vine. The purpose of the vine is to support and provide life giving substance to the branches. When the branches receive its nourishment, it bears fruit or produces fruit.

God is the owner/manager of the vineyard. The vine dresser is an agriculturalist, or a farmer, or a rancher that is involved in the daily pruning and cultivation of grapevines.

So, God the Father is the owner, God the Son is the vine and we, Christians, are the branches. Jesus is the One Who provides all our needs according to His riches and glory in Him. He nourishes us with whatever spiritual gift we need to produce good fruit. He nourishes us with His nature which is the nature of the Father, and through the nature of the Father comes wisdom, strength, character, and all things that keep the plant/church vibrant, energetic, alive and growing. God supplies and Jesus provides.

True Church leaders feed. They do not take away. The vine does not take away the nourishment from the branch, and Church leaders should teach and preach the truth of the Word to their congregation. Jesus asked Peter, *"Do you love Me?"* Peter answered *"Yes,"* then Jesus replied, *"Feed My sheep."* He asked Peter this three times before Peter broke down and cried. We should learn from this lesson because if Jesus reiterated the importance of feeding the sheep three times, then feeding sheep the Word of God is a top priority.

Feeding the sheep is teaching the Word of God. As a mother feeds and protects her child, pastors and teachers are to feed and protect the children of God with the Word of God.

Every branch in Me that does not bear fruit He takes away;

It is the branches job to bear fruit. We, the Church are the branches and we are supposed to bear the good fruit. The fruit we bear should be a sign to this lost world that there is a true God, and Jesus is our Redeemer, our Advocate, our Provider, our Great Shepherd, and He is Faithful and True, and is our Prince of Life, our Horn of Salvation, the Way, The Truth, and the Life, He is the King of kings and the Lord of lords, the Rose of Sharon, the Lily of the Valley – the Son of the True and Living God. It would take all day to list the Names of Jesus but to put it bluntly – He is ALL THAT!

Since we have such a powerful Omnipresent, Omnipotent, and Omniscient Shepherd, His church, we should be bearing love, joy, peace, longsuffering, kindness, goodness, faithfulness, gentleness, and self-control. We as branches need to be the character of the vine which is Christ.

If a tree is not bearing fruit, then it is useless. It is only good for firewood. If we are not bearing good fruit then we are useless. A useless church is a church that meets every week and goes through the motions. There is no spiritual growth and no revelation. Like the Church in Sardis, the branches had a reputation of being alive but they were dead. There's plenty of activity in the Church but no spiritual progress.

As God did with the Church of Sardis, He does to all His churches. He warns them to repent and to get back to the basics of the Gospel of Christ.

We as a Church must have our priorities in order. The Church is in the life saving business, not in the money making business, and if people are not being lead to your church to meet the Master, then there is something wrong. It is easy for the Church to get caught up in the things of the world. We can find an example in John 2: One day, Jesus made a whip and drove all the merchants that were selling oxen, sheep, and doves and the money changers that were doing business in the House of God. He knocked over tables and poured out their money on the ground and said, "Take these things away! Do not make My Father's house a house of merchandise. Jesus did this at the beginning of His ministry and He did it again close to the end of His earthly ministry where Luke records, *"It is written, My house shall be called a house of prayer, but you have made it a den of thieves."* It doesn't matter if your church is decorated with stain glass windows or with card board covering the windows, there should be an utmost respect for the House of God.

And every branch that bears fruit He prunes, that it may bear more fruit.

When we prune our trees and shrubs in the natural, we cut branches away to encourage fuller growth. In order for this to happen, we must cut away all the branches that are unnecessary or unwanted. In the Kingdom of God, we are pruned from time to time to cut out things that are unnecessary or unwanted for Kingdom use. God uses this process to build our spiritual character because we sometimes participate in activities that are not conducive, favorable, helpful, encouraging, advantageous, or beneficial to holy living.

The pruning process is painful but needful. It is a season of cleansing the things in our lives that is causes us to be lethargic, sluggish, or ineffective. It is the small foxes that eat the vine and we have issues in our lives we can do without. If we are lacking in our love walk, the Spirit of the Lord will cause us to interact with someone difficult to demonstrate the love of God in our lives and gives us the grace to love them as God loves us. The Spirit of the Lord does this in all of our discrepancies and shortcomings.

The Lord our God gives us the grace to overcome any and all

obstacles such as lust for money, material things or other character-istics of the flesh. The Lord does this through His pruning process. And when we yield to God's hand in this process, we gradually be-come mature, or perfect in the Lord. This process causes us to be stronger as men and women in Christ.

> *You are already clean because of the word which abides in you. Abide in Me, and I in you. As the branch cannot bear fruit of itself, unless it abides in the vine, neither can you, un-less you abide in Me.*

Jesus calls us clean if we are living by the whole counsel of the Word of God that dwells in us. Without Christ in our lives, we are fruitless at best because it is impossible to live the life of a Christian without Christ. The word Christian means Christ-like and we can-not be Christ-like without Christ. So when we abide, accept, and live in His Word, then we will be well able to bear the fruit of salvation as the Spirit governs our lives.

We will also be able to be sensitive to the voice of God which will di-rect our lives into victorious living. He will keep us from areas that will not be appreciative of the Word. For instance in *Acts 16* Paul wanted to go to Asia, but the Spirit said no. Then he wanted to go to Bithynia, but the Spirit would not permit him. This example surely shows that our steps are ordered from the Lord. Finally, the Spirit permitted him to go to Macedonia where a slave girl was delivered from the kingdom of darkness and a family was saved. We cannot do anything unless we abide in the Word and allow the Word to abide in us.

> *I am the vine, you are the branches. He who abides in Me, and I in him, bears much fruit; for without Me you can do nothing.*

Once again, we take our nourishment from the vine. Just as we must eat physical food for our physical bodies, we must also feed on spiritual food which is the Word of God. In *John 6*, Jesus said that *'I AM the Bread of Life.'*

152

Most assuredly, I say to you, unless you eat the flesh of the Son of Man and drink His blood, you have no life in you. Whoever eats my flesh and drinks My blood has eternal life, and I will raise him up at the last day. For My flesh is food indeed, and My blood is drink indeed. He who eats My flesh and drinks My blood abides in Me, and I in him.

Jesus was speaking figuratively by eating His flesh and drinking His blood. The heart of the matter is when we believe by faith that Jesus is the Son of God, then we believe and walk in His doctrine – we are eating and drinking. How? Because the Word we hear and do becomes a part of us which builds up our spirits as physical food becomes a part of us and build up our bodies. When we walk by faith and not by sight, we are abiding in the Word and the Word is abiding in us.

If anyone does not abide in Me, he is cast out as a branch and is withered, and they gather them and throw them into the fire, and they will be burned.

There are numerous religious bodies that try to operate without Christ, and don't abide in the vine. The results in these bodies without Christ are ones of spiritual disaster. You can tell the characteristics of the Christless churches by their fruits in stealing money from the church to pay bills and house payments, having extra-marital affairs with the opposite sex or even same gender members, the molestation of children, building a doctrine out of context to the Word, sensual dress attire, sensual or provocative praise dances, putting the pastor on a pedestal, gossiping, hating, and unforgiveness rule in these churches. We cannot have a legit church without Christ Jesus as the head of the Church, and not just in Word only, but by our lives. When we abide in the Word, we have eternal life.

When we don't abide in the Word then we are worthless and our only purpose as far as God is concerned is firewood.

153

If you abide in Me, and My words abide in you, you will ask what you desire, and it shall be done for you.

When we stay hungry for the Word of God and continue to hunger and thirst for more of Him, we are abiding. When we read His Word and agree with it, we are abiding. When we walk in the truth of His Word, we are abiding. When we behave as a Christian, then Jesus tells us that we will ask what we desire and it will be done.

There is a trust issue here. The key is abiding in the Word of God. When we are abiding in the Word of God – then we will be asking for things that will elevate the Word of God in our lives and in the lives of others. We won't be driven by selfish ambition and lustful living as the world does. The new nature in you will be driven by a righteous integrity that is led by the Holy Spirit. And because you are in right standing with the Lord and your decisions and request will align with Him.

By this My Father is glorified, that you bear much fruit; so you will be My disciples.

God is glorified when we live right and represent Him as we should. He will work with us as He did with Jesus to bring in our portion of the harvest. Then we will hear Him say, *"Well done thy good and faithful servant."*

Notes:

Chapter 14

That Religious Bunch

Dark Plots

It is no strange thing for the works of darkness to pick or choose its time, or occasions in time, to do its dark and dirty deeds. *Luke 4:13* records the devil leaving Jesus because his attempt to cause Him to fail had failed and he couldn't get Him to sin even in His weaken condition (physically). You remember the story; Jesus had spent forty days and forty nights in the wilderness to be tempted by the devil. He was in the hot sun all day and in the chilly desert air all night for forty days. He did not eat anything during this period and at the end of the forty days, Satan thought that he might be able to sway the King of kings and the Lord of lords in His weaken condition. So he approached our Lord, and tried to appeal to Him in His state of physical famishment.

However, with every attempt he tried to cause Jesus to sin, Satan was disappointed when he heard these three words three times, *"It is written!"* There is nothing stronger than the Word of God. The Word of God creates, destroys, and does whatever commands that flow from the Master's lips. This is truly a sword for all Christian men and women to use when we are under attack by the enemy. *"It is written!"* The Word of God will always prevail over the attacks of the enemy. As Jesus taught by example, we should study His examples so that when hard times come, we would be equipped with the Word of God and send the devil packing as Jesus did.

Now, just because the devil left Him does not mean he will never come back. The Bible tells us Satan decided to leave Him and wait for a more opportune time to try his tactics in getting Him to sin against God. As Satan watched Jesus, he also watches us. He studies us to discover our likes and dislikes. He will try to use what we like to bring us into bondage again. For instance, if a man takes a second glance at a woman, whether she is well endowed, beautiful, skinny, pigeon-toed, cross-eyed or hippy, the devil will take note of that and will send you a steady diet across your path. He studies your weaknesses so that he can take advantage of you when you least expect it. He realizes he has to catch us off guard because that is where he has the greatest chance to manipulate us.

Here is an example from the Bible. One of the most interesting stories is one of the infamous Judas Iscariot – the perfect hypocrite. Judas was one of the twelve disciples. And as a disciple he watched Jesus feed the multitude, heal the sick, raise the dead, cleanse lepers, walk on water, cast out demons, and calm the storm many times. He also went out when Jesus commissioned him to preach, *"The Kingdom of Heaven is at Hand."* He was active in healing the sick, cleansing lepers, raising the dead, and casting out demons. After witnessing all these events, and participating in them, you would think that Judas would be strong in the Lord and in the power of His might. You would think he would be an authority of Christ. However the truth is he spent time with the Light, but he did not embrace the light.

We can find an example in *John 12*, when Jesus and the disciples were at Bethany where Lazarus and his sisters lived. Jesus had already raised Lazarus from the dead and they were having dinner together. Then Mary took a very costly oil of spikenard and anointed the Master's feet.

But when Judas saw what was done he said, *"Why was this fragrant not sold for three hundred denarii and given to the poor?"* Now a denarius was the denominational coin of currency which was the wages for a days' labor, [See *Matthew 20:2*] So three-hundred denarius was basically a year's wages. The Bible says that Judas did not care for the poor but was a thief who happened to be the treasurer, for he kept dipping in the money box. This was stealing the Church money for your own personal use. What was meant for the poor was spent on himself. If you are a deacon in your church and you are taking money to pay your rent, car bill, utilities, or the casino, you are a thief with the same spirit of Judas.

1 Timothy 6:9-10
But those who desire to be rich fall into temptation and a snare, and many foolish and harmful lusts which drown men in destruction and perdition. For the love of money is a root of all evil, for which some have strayed from the faith in their greediness, and pierced themselves through with many sorrows.

Judas is a prime example of not pressing for the prize of the high calling of God and allowing, or giving place to Satan. Judas was trying to play both ends as a disciple of Christ but he had dark desires for money. He is a prime example of having a form of godliness, but denying the power thereof. But he is not the only one, there are millions of people who say they are Christians on Sunday morning, but they dabble with darkness all week long. Jesus says that *we cannot serve two masters; we will either love the one or hate the other or we will either be loyal to one or despise the other.* We either love Jesus and the doctrine of Christ or we will despise Him and His doctrine of life. There are many churches that will have to take a stand on the Word of God, or we will find ourselves as Judas found himself. We have to have the heart, the will, and respect for God to operate as the Bible teaches us to operate. For if these things are not in our hearts, then we will be lackadaisical in our walk with the Lord and will eventually leave doors open for the enemy to come in and make himself at home as he did with Judas.

Matthew 12:43
When an unclean spirit goes out of a man, he goes through dry places, seeking rest, and finds none. Then he says, 'I will return to my house from which I came.' And when he comes, he finds it empty, swept, and put in order. Then he goes and takes with him seven other spirits more wicked than himself, and they enter and dwell there, and the last state of that man is worse than the first. So shall it also be with this wicked generation.

In the Scripture above, an unclean spirit was cast out of a man. The man was free from demonic activity because he was swept and clean. However, the man did nothing to protect himself (being filled by the Spirit of God) from further attacks from the enemy. He probably rejoiced and went to parties and celebrated his freedom and in all of that, he left a door open.

We have locks and security systems on our houses, on our cars, and on all things we hold dear. But we don't have locks, security systems on ourselves unless we are abiding in the Word.

Now after the spirit left, it went around looking for a new place to live, another body to possess, but couldn't find one and got homesick. He remembered how he was kicked out of that body because he was not strong enough to hold the fort down. He was not strong enough to maintain his house, (a human body). So he went and picked up other spirits that were worse, far more wicked and filthier than he was. So he enlisted their services and they all went into the swept and clean house and took over. Now he was eight times worse than he was before.

Judas was swept and cleaned also when Jesus chose him to be His disciple, the treasurer, and His betrayer. Jesus knew who Judas was and who he would become, but He loved him anyway and taught him along with the eleven, the ways of righteousness. But Judas was operating in the darkness as a part time job even when he walked with Jesus. A little sin here and a little sin there can and will eventually take you down a road to where you are lost in your thinking, sketchy in your actions, false actions of love, a place where confusion of what is right and what is wrong retards the person, becomes erroneous in spiritual matters, and blind in common sense. Judas was an easy possession because for Satan he was already operating in the kingdom of darkness, masquerading as a disciple of light. He was worshipping Satan through his thoughts and his actions and he paid the wages for his sins.

But Judas was not by himself. Over the years, the religious groups had gotten off track because they were lost and didn't respect God or His Son. When a person disbelieves the Son, he/she comes against the Father. Disobedience and unbelief will do that. When God is pushed aside in our hearts, then carnal pride and self-establishment will replace the void within them. Then they become their own man and have become "somebody." People love being somebody. They had power, (by human standards), and power generally has a tendency to corrupt a person and flood their souls with the attributes of darkness. The Pharisees, Sadducees and the Scribes had these character traits and it was these people that Jesus often rebuked. Why? Because of their hypocrisy of false worship or false dedication to God. They served Him with their lips and not their hearts.

> *John 11:45*
> *Then many of the Jews who had come to Mary, and had seen the things Jesus did, believed in Him. But some of them went away to the Pharisees and told them the things Jesus did. Then the chief priest and the Pharisees gathered a council and said, "What shall we do? For this man works many signs. If we let Him alone like this, everyone will believe in Him and the Romans will come and take away both our place and nation."*

They were nervous and held a board meeting to discuss the problem they had with Jesus. They were scared of losing their place of notoriety because Jesus was becoming too popular. People believed in Him because of the things He was doing, raising the dead, cleansing lepers, healing the sick, feeding the multitudes, giving the Good News of salvation to the down and trodden. The religious groups could not compete with that. So in the mind of darkness, what could not be controlled must be killed.

In the 23rd chapter of Matthew, Jesus rebuked the religious establishment over their false dedication to God and their conceitedness.

> *"But all their works they do to be seen by men. They make their phylacteries broad and enlarge the boarders of their garments. They love the best places at feast, the best seats in the synagogues, greetings in the marketplaces, and to be called by men, 'Rabbi, Rabbi.'"*

Their positions were in danger and something had to be done about it. They couldn't afford losing their status with the people. They would miss the pat on their backs, their greetings in the marketplace, and would be taking a back seat in all the feasts and lose the prestige of being called Rabbi. They were afraid and this good ol' boy system had to make a decision to kill the competition, kill the move of God so they could be comfortable.

When they first heard the Words of life and light, they marveled at the wonderful Words that flowed from His lips, but after a while they began plotting ways to kill Him. Why? Their hearts were exposed due to doubt and unbelief. The light always exposes the hearts and deeds of the darkness. He told the truth about their desires and the motivation for their actions. Did they thank Him for it? No, in return, they wanted to kill Him at all cost. Positive or constructive criticism was not in their by-laws. In fact, there were numerous attempts to trick Him, and they were constantly on watch trying to catch Him saying something contrary to the Law of Moses so they could kill Him according to the law.

The Bible tells us that Satan entered Judas and he went to the established religious authority with a deal to turn Jesus over to them. When the chief priest and captains heard the plot of betrayal by His own, they were happy and overjoyed. The Jews were delighted and promised Judas Iscariot monetary value which was thirty pieces of silver. One of the conditions was to turn Him in when the crowd was not around. They wanted Jesus arrested secretly and privately absent of the crowd. They feared the people because a lot of them believed in Jesus as either a great Prophet or the Son of God. So Judas, like his father Satan, waited for an opportune time to betray Him.

Judas finally got his chance on the Day of the Unleavened Bread; when the Passover must be killed. After Jesus washed the feet of the disciples, He gave a lesson on servanthood. Then He said, *"Most assuredly, I say to you, one of you will betray Me."* All the disciples got nervous when He made the announcement. They were perplexed, confounded, baffled as they looked at one another, trying to figure out who He was talking about.

John was leaning on Jesus bosom and Peter motioned to him to ask which one of them will do such a horrible thing. Peter is one of the most colorful and illustrated of the twelve and there is no telling what he was thinking. He may have been thinking of cutting or cursing the one who would do a terrible thing as this. But the Bible does not say what Peter's intentions were except to find out who would be the one that would betray the Hope of Glory. So John asked Jesus who it would be.

> *John 13:26-27*
> *Jesus answered, "It is he to whom I shall give a piece of bread when I have dipped it." And having dipped the bread, He gave it to Judas Iscariot, the son of Simon. Now after the piece of bread, Satan entered him. Then Jesus said to him, "What you do, do quickly."*

Later that night, after Jesus prayed the prayer in *John 17*, Judas led a detachment of troops, and officers from the chief priest and Pharisees. They carried lanterns, torches and weapons to arrest the Savior of the World as if He were a common crook or a villain, or a criminal. But Jesus knew all that would happen to Him, He was the Son of God, and He had prophesied to His Prophets, kings, and priest through the years of this night and now it was time to fulfill them.

Notes:

Notes:

Chapter 15
Foretold

Like He Said He Would

God always tells the story before it is lived out. He told Abraham his children would be in bondage for over four hundred years and they were. He told him they would be a great nation and they are. He told him that Ishmael would also be a great nation and they are. He foretold the deliverance of Israel from Egypt. He foretold the coming of Josiah, the boy king who would tear down the altars of Baal and he did. He told Isaiah about the coming of John the Baptist and the Messiah and they came.

One of the most wonderful things about Christ was His accuracy on future events. During His mission He told His disciples He would die and would rise again. In *Matthew 17*, Jesus disclosed information on future events concerning Himself.

> *Indeed, Elijah is coming first and will restore all things. But I say to you that Elijah has come already, and they did not know him but did to him whatever they wished. Likewise the Son of Man is also about to suffer at their hands."*

The Bible tells us John the Baptist will go before The Christ in the spirit and power of Elijah. This prophecy was fulfilled in part, Elijah did come back to fulfill the prophecy of John the Baptist. It is very possible that Elijah will complete this prophesy during the time of the two witnesses in *Revelation 3-6*.

They did not know John the Baptist as Elijah however, they could have recognized him through the Old Testament, but they didn't.

As you know, John rebuked Herod for marrying his brother's wife who is also his niece. For this reason, John the Baptist was put in jail and was eventually beheaded. Jesus tells His disciples that He will also suffer in the hands of men.

> *Mark 8:31*
>
> *And He began to teach them that the Son of Man must suffer many things, and be rejected by the elders and chief priest and scribes, and be killed, after three days rise again. He spoke this word openly, then Peter took Him aside and began to rebuke Him, but when He turned around and looked at the disciples, He rebuked Peter, saying, "Get behind Me Satan! For you are not mindful of the things of God, but of the things of man."*

This was just one of several predictions Jesus made concerning Himself. He was rejected by the elders, chief priest, and scribes because they did not understand. They did not want to understand because Jesus threatened their way of life, their prestigious living, and their selfish ways of serving God. They loved the approval of the ignorant crowd rather than loving God in Spirit and in Truth.

When Peter heard this, he was genuinely appalled because he was looking at the situation naturally instead of spiritually. He had just declared Jesus was the Christ and now Christ announced He would be killed. He didn't see this as a work from God, nor could he because the Holy Spirit hadn't opened his eyes of understanding. Peter and several others believed that Christ would come to liberate Israel from the Romans and rule the world. However, Peter did not understand that Jesus did not come to initiate a physical kingdom but a Spiritual Kingdom for the benefit of man. The Kingdom of God would be within man, according to Jesus in *Luke 17:21*.

Peter was upset and tried to rebuke the King of kings and Lord of lords. He believed that Jesus is the Son of God and could not be defeated in any way, form, or fashion. His line of thinking was how can the creation kill the Creator? He thought Jesus was wrong, incorrect, erroneous, and out of line in this declaration.

But Jesus looked at him and said, *"Get behind Me Satan! For you are not mindful of the things of God, but of the things of men."* I'll bet Peter's heart sunk in his chest when he heard the Master's rebuke and calling him Satan. Peter did not understand Jesus came to earth to die for the sins of man and to set us straight. Peter did not know Jesus came to open the hearts of men in order to become the family of God.

Mark 9:31
The Son of Man is being betrayed into the hands of men, and they will kill Him, and after He is killed, He will rise the third day.

Again Jesus predicted to be betrayed, killed, buried and raised on the third day

Matthew 17:22
Now while they were staying in Galilee, Jesus said to them, (disciples), "The Son of Man is about to be betrayed into the hands of men, and they will kill Him, and the third day He will raise up." And they (disciples) were exceedingly sorrowful.

When Jesus told them He would be betrayed into the hands of men, the disciples didn't really understand what He was saying. I believe Judas did not have a clue at this point he would be the one to betray Him. He may have been busy looking at the opportunities to get personal gain. The disciples were not spiritual men yet, they were still carnal or natural men for they had not received the Holy Spirit as of yet.

Now Jesus had been betrayed by Judas Iscariot as He said He would. The disciples scattered as He said they would. Peter denied Jesus three times as He said he would. He was rejected by the Sanhedrin which consisted of the elders, Pharisees, Sadducees, the chief priest and scribes who had Him beaten beyond recognition, beyond the semblance of a man like He said He would. He hung on the cross, committed His spirit into the hands of the Father and died like He said He would.

165

After the death of Christ, Joseph of Arimathea and Nicodemas, who were both members of the council but were not in agreement with the killing of Jesus, took His body and anointed Him with one hundred pounds of a mixture of aloes and myrrh. Then they laid Jesus in the tomb.

Jesus made the prediction about His death and resurrection openly and others heard what He said. So the day after His death, the chief priest, and the Pharisees went to Pilate and told him that deceiver (Jesus) predicted to rise from the dead in three days.

Matthew 27:64
"Therefore command that the tomb be made secure until the third day, lest His disciples come by night and steal Him away, and say to the people, 'He has risen from the dead,' so the last deception will be worse than the first."

One distinctive trait about the kingdom of darkness is nervousness of the unknown. They heard Jesus say, *"three days and I will rise"* and they were hoping and praying His statement would be false. They were also worried about the disciples stealing Him away from the tomb and claim He has risen.

Pilate said to them, *"You have a guard, go your way, and make it as secure as you know how."* So they went and made the tomb secure, sealing the stone and setting the guard. They thought they were secure. However, at the breaking of the dawn on the first day of the week, an angel came from Heaven and rolled the stone away from the door and he sat on the giant rock that was formally sealed. The angel did not roll the stone away for Christ to come out, but for others to see He was not in there.

Regardless how bad they treated Jesus, and beat Jesus, and clowned Jesus; regardless of how they sealed the tomb and placed guards there to keep others out but that One in - And still Jesus rose from the dead – like He said He would.

Chapter 16

Born of God

The Sin Problem
Matthew 1:21
And she will bring forth a Son, and you shall call His name Jesus, for He will save His people from their sins.

The plan of God was to provide salvation for those He chose even before the foundation of the earth. When the fullness of time came, Jesus was born according to the Scripture, lived according to the Scriptures, did mighty acts according to the Scriptures and did not commit a single sin according to the Scriptures. He lived a sinless life to save the world from sin.

> *Romans 3:23*
> *For all have sinned and fall short of the glory of God.*

Everyone on the planet has sinned at one time (or many times) or another. We all were born with a sin nature and we kept that sin nature until we sincerely accepted Christ Jesus as Lord and Savior. As I pointed out earlier, we were natural born thieves, liars, and carried a host of other carnal personality traits which was in our DNA at birth.

> *Ephesians 2:8-9*
> *For by grace you have been saved through faith, and that not of yourselves; it is the gift from God, not of works, lest anyone should boast.*

Salvation is a free gift from God. We can't buy the gift of salvation as some religions and cults proclaim. We cannot work our way into Heaven although once we are saved – we will have a work to do in His Kingdom. There are many church members who attend services every Sunday and Wednesday who believe these actions will get them into Heaven. Singing in the choir won't get you to Heaven, even preaching the Gospel won't get you there if your heart is not right. Sacrificing bulls, goats, turtle doves and sheep will not get us into Heaven. Contrary to popular belief, the Pope cannot get you into Heaven through praying the prayer that addresses, "Mary, mother of God." It is only through Christ Jesus, the Son of God; we can obtain salvation and Heaven.

It is by grace we are saved. Grace, God's divine influence upon the hearts of men is the central key to salvation for God chose us, we did not choose Him. God knows the end from the beginning and the beginning to the end. He knew who would receive His salvation through His divine, heavenly, and deific influence. He knew who would receive His Son, Jesus the Messiah, Jesus the Christ as their personal Lord and Savior.

It is by faith in what Jesus did at the cross that makes our salvation possible. There will not be one person standing before God who did not get there through and by Jesus.

We are saved by grace through faith in Christ Jesus our Lord. One of the things that drive me batty is hearing my brothers and sisters declare, "I'm a sinner saved by grace." We're not sinners any longer. When Christ died on the cross – He died for all our sins. So we are either sinners or we are saved by grace. It's one of the two.

> *Romans 5:8*
> *But God demonstrates His love toward us, in that while we were still sinners, Christ died for us.*

While we were yet still sinners, while we were acting out, stealing, killing, having sex all over the place, lying, coveting, and worshipping other gods, Christ died for us. We didn't know who we were, but Christ knew who we were and died for all of our sins. It doesn't matter what we have done, what sins we have committed, whether telling a lie or killing a million people, Jesus Christ took the punishment for our sins, and not only ours – but the whole world.

We were dealt a bad hand due to Adam's disobedience, so God demonstrated, established, validated, and confirmed His love for us by sending His only begotten Son to die for our sins and to purchase a place in Heaven for us.

> *Romans 6:1-4*
> *What shall we say then? Shall we continue in sin that grace may abound? Certainly not! How shall we who died to sin live any longer in it? Or do you not know that as many of us as were baptized into Christ Jesus were baptized into death? Therefore we were buried with Him through baptism into death that just as Christ was raised from the dead by the glory of the Father, even so we should walk in newness of life.*

There are some who believe we can keep on sinning. They believe we can keep on lying, keep on stealing, keep on killing, keep on worshipping other gods, keep on hating our brothers and sisters, keep on gossiping, keep on committing adultery, keep on playing with witchcraft (or supporting it), keep on being jealous, keep on displaying outburst of wrath, continue in our selfish ambition, in heresies, in drunkenness, in lewdness, in uncleanness, in dissensions, and in revelries, and believe that God's grace is sufficient. We are missing the point, just because we are under God's grace doesn't mean we have a license to sin. What we do have now is the power not to sin.

When we were baptized into Christ, (that is brought under into His death), we were buried or submerged with Him in His death. We were also buried with Him, which means we have died to sin and when Christ was raised from death, we were raised also with the results of our freedom from sin. Now we can walk in the newness of life. Our old sin life (nature) has passed away and now we are able to live a sinless life. We need to receive this truth in our spirit so we can walk it out in our life.

Romans 6:5-6

For if we have been united together in the likeness of His death, certainly we also shall be in the likeness of His resurrection, knowing this that our old man was crucified with Him, that the body of sin might be done away with, that we should no longer be slaves to sin.

We are no longer slaves to sin. We are no longer sin kings and queens in the kingdom of darkness. We no longer have a hook in our jaw that compels us to sin against our bodies and God. We are no longer helpless, abandoned, deserted, stranded, or high and dry – Christ bought our freedom from sin with His perfect blood that we may be perfect in Him.

vs 10-11

For the death that He died, He died to sin once and for all; but the life that He lives, He lives to God. Likewise, you also reckon yourselves to be dead indeed to sin, but alive to God in Christ Jesus our Lord.

There is no do over here! Jesus died one time for our sins and the life He lives is for God. Since Jesus died for our sins and abolished them, we should as Christian men and women reckon ourselves or envision, picture, conceive, consider, or regard that we also are dead to sin but alive to God. When Jesus abolished sin, He eliminated, obliterated and stopped sin in our lives. Remember, no sin can approach God but since we are dead to sin, we have right standing with the Father. We are alive in the True and Living God.

To be dead to sin is like a dead man in a casket; you can slap the dead man, shoot the dead man, stab the dead man or even set him on fire. Does the dead man respond? No he doesn't because he is dead. He cannot feel the slap, the bullet, the knife or even the fire for he is dead. We should be like dead men when it comes to sin, we are not affected, not influenced, and not partial to sin in our lives. Christ declared we are dead to sin because we have a new nature, the very nature of God dwelling in us and it acts like a sin repellent in our lives. We are dead to stealing, dead to killing, dead to raping, dead to fighting, dead to drugs, dead to fornication, dead to homosexuality; we are dead to the world. The old man is dead!

When Satan tries to influence us into sin, we now have the power to say no. We now have the power to say, *"It is written,"* We have the power to live a sinless life for the rest of our days because the nature of God the Father, God the Son and God the Holy Spirit has taken up residence in our bodies, in out spirit. The new man is alive and free not to sin.

Ephesians 1: 7
In Him we have redemption through His blood, the forgiveness of sins, according to the riches of His grace.

Again, we are redeemed, bought back, converted from the kingdom of darkness by the blood of Jesus the Messiah. We now have forgiveness of all our sins according to His bountiful, munificent, magnanimous, generous, and plentiful riches of His grace.

Hebrews 10:26
For if we sin willingly after we have received the knowledge of the truth, there no longer remains a sacrifice for sins.

If a person gives his life to Christ, is baptized and born-again, has been taught the ways of the covenant and received the knowledge of the truth, but go back to a life of sin, then he has done the worst possible thing in the world. To return to a sin filled life will be spiritual suicide. There no longer remains a sacrifice for sins. For you, Jesus died for nothing, He was beaten for nothing, He was whipped for nothing, and He gave up His Spirit at the cross for nothing.

Satan will also try to implant pop-ups in your mind of bad deeds in your history. We have to put these pop-ups to rest immediately and we must refuse to dwell on our bad history. If you dwell on these thoughts (pop-ups), you will be back in the game of death before too long. Remember, they are not your thoughts; they are the thoughts of Satan trying to lure you back in his kingdom. Also remember, if you do take heed to these extreme thoughts, you will be eight times worse than you were before you were delivered.

Hebrews 6:4-6
For it is impossible for those who were once enlighten, and have tasted the heavenly gift, and have become partakers of the Holy Spirit, and have tasted the good word of God and the powers to come, if they fall away, to renew them again to repentance, since they crucify again for themselves the Son of God, and put Him to open shame.

Jesus willingly, eagerly, and freely gave His life for mankind to save us from our sins and made it possible for us to live a life without sin. Why would anyone want to go back to a dreaded lifestyle of sin and darkness where blindness, confusion, rebellion, spiritual error and ignorance are chief character traits?

If a person falls away and goes back to a life of sin after he has learned the truth, there will not be a comeback for this person. There will be no repentance for this person – they are gone.

1 John 2:19
They went out from us, but they were not of us; for if they had been of us, they would have continued with us, but they went out that they might be made manifest, that none of them were of us.

Believe it or not, everyone on the planet does not want Jesus in their lives. There are people that you would bend over backwards for and they will stab you in the back for your efforts. This is one of the main characteristics of the kingdom of darkness. And people in this kingdom just do not want to leave their life of sin. They enjoy the misery of bondage to sin and even though it will cost them their lives – we find they just live for the moment and not the future.

There are a millions of people who have joined a Christ-centered church for a season. I believe most were just curious to see what goes on in the Church. They would stay awhile, make an assessment and depart. The bottom line is they were with us but they left us – they really did not hold the Lord Jesus in their hearts. They were there physically but not spiritually. Their body was in the church building, but their minds were in the world.

> *John 8:34*
> *Jesus answered them, "Most assuredly, I say to you, whoever commits sin is a slave to sin.*

If you are still sinning, you are a slave to sin. A slave has no rights, and is captive without the possibility of a life of freedom. Sinners are actually drawn to sin and cannot help themselves because sin has locked them down. Many times a little sin here and a little sin there will cause you to escalate into a life of sin, and even crime. Some believe they can master sin, only to find out they are mastered by sin and have become enslaved in sin.

There are some that want to live right, but without Jesus, it is impossible to live a life without sin without Jesus as your Lord and Savior. There are millions of people who live valiantly, nobly, and courageously but without Christ – they're common sinners. And whoever commits sin is a slave to sin.

> *2 Corinthians 5:21*
> *For He made Him who knew no sin to be sin for us, that we might become the righteousness of God in Him.*

God made The Holy One, Jesus, Who knew no sin to be sin. Jesus never committed a sin in His life. He did not have sex with anyone; He never did an unclean act, or a lewd act. Jesus never lied, stole, cheated or dabbled with sorcery. He wasn't jealous of anyone, never caused dissensions or spoke heresies or practiced selfish ambition. He didn't murder anyone or took part in revelries (wild parties).

Jesus had to be the perfect sacrifice in order to deliver us from the kingdom of darkness into the Kingdom of Light. He took the sins of the world out of our lives and became sin in our place. The punishment we as the human race deserved was given to the king of Kings and the Lord of lords. He took every wrong act and wrong thought we had and did and died for us. This is like standing in front of a judge for the crimes of murder, kidnapping, rape, lying, stealing, and the whole nine yards. We were actually and factually guilty as charged and when the judge was about to pronounce judgment and sentence upon us – Jesus stood in the courtroom and took our charges and the punishment for our crimes. The innocent for the guilty.

There had to be a perfect sacrifice and Jesus was the perfect One. He was without any blemishes, faults, spots, wrinkles, imperfections, stains, or blotches. He was perfect in every way. But God made Him sin that we might be saved and made the righteousness of God in Christ Jesus.

He abolished sin so we can live a sinless life after we repent of our sins and ask the Holy One to come into our lives. When this happens we are brand new creatures, with a new DNA from God. We are now born of God and the old life, the old way of living has been taken away and we are able to live in the newness of life. We are able to live a life without sin.

This is hard to swallow for a lot of people. They do not see God in the proper light of His Word. Instead of looking at God and what He promised us, and what He did for us, and what He is doing for us now – we look at ourselves in low esteem, in low reverence, in low regard, in low honor and low approval. These thoughts are self-destructive and hogwash from the devil and millions of people have fallen into this trap and made it a way of life. The truth about these thoughts is they are an act of false humility and rebellion against God.

God will let you believe what you want to believe. He has given us His Word, He has given us His Son and we have a choice to believe the truth of God or our own stinking thinking. Jesus died for our sins so that we can live without sin. This was God's plan all along and it is up to us to follow the plan. It is up to us to agree with God in all points and when we do, His promises are yes and amen.

Every act of sin brings us closer to the Day of the Lord.

1 John 1:5
This is the message which we have heard from Him and declare to you, that God is light and in Him is no darkness at all.

As we have declared throughout this book, God is light, the epitome of light and it is impossible for any shred of darkness to penetrate Him, manipulate Him, influence Him, blind Him, enter Him, equal Him or overcome Him. God is the Rock of rocks as He is the Father of the King of kings and darkness cannot cause His light to go dim, or shadowy, or blurry, vague, hazy, or faint. When the Light comes, darkness is defeated and demolished and has to flee.

There is no darkness in the light, and there is no darkness in God the Father, God the Son or God the Holy Spirit.

vs 6-7
If we say we have fellowship with Him, and walk in darkness, we lie and do not practice the truth. But if we walk in the light as He is in the light, we have fellowship with one another and the blood of Jesus Christ His Son cleanses us from all sin.

If we say we are Christian and participate in adultery, open sex with whosoever, uncleanness, vulgarity, profanity, unwholesomeness, idolatry, sorcery (which is witchcraft), hatred, arguments, disputes, jealousies, outburst of wrath, selfish ambitions, rebellions, conflicts, dissents, heresies, envy, murders drunkenness, and revelries then we are a liar and do not practice the truth.

However, when we live and communicate and exist in the love of God and walk in His ways, then we have fellowship with one another. One of the key points in Christianity is walking in love, and fellowship with one another. When we exhibit this lifestyle, *the blood of Jesus cleanses us from all sin.* So when He cleanses us from all sin, then we have no sin!

v 9

If we say that we have no sin, we deceive ourselves , and the truth is not in us. If we confess our sins, He is faithful and just to forgive us our sins and to cleanse us from all unrighteousness.

Everyone on the planet has sinned; we were all sinners until we came into the knowledge of Christ so now we are saints and not sinners. This verse is very clear, when we confess our sins, Jesus is able to forgive our sins and cleanse us from all unrighteousness or bad, sinful and terrible acts. Notice it reads, Jesus is able to cleanse us from all unrighteousness or sin. When we are cleansed we are washed and purified. When we are cleansed the sin we had is no more. God says He will not remember them, no matter how many times you have sinned. The Bible says Gods throws our sins in the Sea of Forgetfulness. In *Jeremiah 31:35b*, God says, *"I will forgive their iniquity and their sin I will remember no more."* And in *Psalms 103:21* God says, *"As far as the East is from the West, so far He has removed our transgressions from us."* How far is the east from the west? I don't know either but God says He will forgive us our sins and remember them no more. Furthermore in *The Book of Micah*, it states that He throws our sins in the Sea of Forgetfulness.

v 10

If we say that we have not sinned, we make Him a liar, and His word is not in us.

We have all sinned in the past. If we say we have not sinned, we are in terrible and dangerous trouble as liars because we were born in sin and lived in sin until we received the salvation of Christ Jesus our Lord. God said we have sinned and if we disagree with that, then we call God a liar and His Word cannot be in us. I believe it would be best if we weren't ever born than to call God a liar.

1 John 2:1
My little children, these things I write to you, so that you

may not sin. And if anyone sins, we have an Advocate with the Father, Jesus Christ the righteous.

John says he writes to us so that we may not sin. The term, *"may not sin,"* informs us that it is possible for a Christian to sin. Even though we are born-again, have the nature of God in us – we can still decide to sin. We would have to think about it, meditate on it, contemplate over it, reason, consider and ponder over it. And when we have made a decision, we would have to ignore the Holy Spirit that dwells in us before we do the deed. We would have to turn our back on God to go about doing the deed.

Then there are times when we may get into the flesh and sin. Our flesh and The Spirit that dwells with us are at war. Our flesh is of the earth but our spirit is from God. The Bible teaches us that our flesh will always be against God. However, if we do sin we have an advocate, a supporter, a sponsor, a lawyer, who will go to the Father for you and intercede.

v 2
And He Himself is the propitiation for our sins, and not ours only but for the whole world.

Propitiation is an appeasement, or pacification or a substitute. So Jesus is our propitiation, or appeasement, or our pacification to God for our sins. Jesus was our substitute at the cross, it should had been us at the cross but Jesus took our place, took the punishment for the crimes/sins we were guilty of. He appeased the Father on our behalf, He is our reconciler and He is the ultimate lawyer Who has never lost a case. Jesus did not die just for the Church, but for the whole world. Every person in the world has the chance to believe in Christ Jesus, The Holy One of God.

1 John 3:1-2
Behold what matter of love the Father has bestowed on us, that we should be called children of God! Therefore the world

*does not know us, because it did not know Him. Beloved, now
we are children of God; and it has not yet been revealed what
we shall be, but we know that when He is revealed, we shall be
like Him, for we shall see Him as He is.*

It is truly a blessing that we have the love of the Father. There is
no greater love than the love the Father has for His children. This love
separates us from the rest of the world because God has made us His
chosen people, a holy nation, a royal priesthood, His special people, because He brought us out of the darkness into His own marvelous light.

Have you ever wondered why the world is so crazy, out of bal-
ance, hateful and disoriented? Because they are of the world and
don't know God. They have an idea of 'a god' but they don't know
the True and Living God. Since the world does not know God they
also do not truly know Christians or the sons of God. Remember
when Jesus came into the world, the world did not know Him, so
the world does not know us. There have been numerous times in
life's history where if something is not understood, men will try to
dismiss it, conquer it or kill it.

It will be a great day when we see Jesus face to face, but when we
finally see Him, the Bible says that we will be like Him. Amen!

v 3
*And everyone who has this hope in Him purifies himself,
just as He is pure.*

To purify ourselves is to let go of everything that is not of God
and embrace everything that is of God. We also need to refrain
from the little foxes, the small questionable activities that has the
possibility to grow into full fledge sin. We should all have this hope
and we should all purify ourselves just as Jesus was/is pure. We are
to spread the Gospel and not get tangled in the sins of the world.

1 Peter 2:1-5
Therefore, laying aside all malice, all deceit, hypocrisy, envy,

and all evil speaking, as new born babes, desire the pure milk of the word, that you may grow thereby, if indeed you have tasted that the Lord is gracious. Coming to Him as to a living stone, rejected indeed by men, but chosen by God and precious, you also, as living stones are being built up a spiritual house, a holy priesthood, to offer up spiritual sacrifices acceptable to God through Jesus Christ.

We must forsake all malice, hatred, nastiness, wickedness, and mischievousness in our lives. We must not practice any form of deceit, dishonesty, treachery, pretense, and trickery any longer for it is not the character of new creations in Christ Jesus. We must speak with pure conversation, uplifting, encouraging and speaking the truth and not falsehoods.

Desiring the pure milk of the Word is craving the Word, being eager for the Word, being thirsty for the Word and this will cause you to grow. However, you must believe, ingest it, and you will surely grow into maturity. The men of the world reject us, but God has chosen us to be living stones to build us up to a spiritual house, (the body of Christ). We offer up our sacrifices by selflessly doing the will of God, by living the will of God in obedience to His Word.

> *vs 4-5*
> *Whoever commits sin also commits lawlessness, and sin is lawlessness. And you know that He was manifested to take away our sins, and in Him there is no sin.*

Whoever premeditates, plans, strategies, contemplates, anticipates, and envisions to sin commits lawlessness. The whole world was at this point in one form or another before Christ came with the gift of salvation. He was manifested to take away the sins of the world and He did it at the cross.

> *v 6*
> *Whoever abides in Him does not sin. Whoever sins has*

neither seen Him nor known Him.

Whoever fellowships, communes, obeys, submits and conform to sin is not in Christ. Christ does not sin. Sin and Holiness cannot get along for they are incompatible, unsuited, unharmonious, and discordant. Whoever practices sin or wrong doing simply does not know God.

vs 7-8
Little children, let no one deceive you. He who practices righteousness is righteous, just as He is righteous. He who sins is of the devil, for the devil has sinned from the beginning. For this purpose the Son of God was manifested, that He might destroy the works of the devil.

As mentioned in an earlier chapter on bearing fruit, if you are practicing righteousness then you are righteous as Jesus is righteous, or you are bearing good fruit. If you are practicing unrighteousness, then you are living a sinful life and partner with the devil who has been sinning before the beginning of time. It is for this reason God sent Jesus into the world, so that He would destroy the works of the devil.

v 9
Whoever has been born of God does not sin, for His seed remains in him; and he cannot sin, because he has been born of God.

This is as clear as you can get, if you are born of God, you will not live a life of sin for His nature is in you. If God's nature is in you – you cannot sin because we are born of God. There is no such thing as a sinning Christian, just as there is no such thing as a holy devil. So every Christian on the planet should wrap this revelation around their brain, we are born of God so we do not sin.

Do not make excuses for this verse as some do. We cannot look at this verse and verses like it from our minds; we should take this as Gospel because it is Gospel. We need to destroy the opinion of ourselves in our minds and start agreeing with what the Bible says about us. We need to dump, delete, obliterate, remove, and erase our carnal thinking, which is stinking thinking, and come into agreement with God's thoughts – we need to switch from an unrighteous state of mind to a righteous state of mind. The devil tells people this type of thinking is sin, we're not God and we are flesh and blood and therefore cannot do this. But the devil is a liar and he wants your soul to share hell with him forever.

> *v 10*
> *In this the children of God and the children of the devil are manifest: Whoever does not practice righteousness is not of God, nor is he who does not love his brother.*

Notes:

Notes:

Chapter 17

The Church

Bishops/Pastors/Elders

The Church is a collection of God's children throughout the earth. The building where people congregate to worship God and to hear His Word is called a church; however, the truth of the matter is the people are the Church. It is the people of God that comprises His Church and He set guidelines for us to follow in order to have a healthy Church body.

> *This is a faithful saying: If a man desires the position of a bishop, he desires a good work. A bishop then must be blameless, the husband of one wife, temperate, sober minded, of good behavior, hospitable, able to teach, not given to wine, not violent, not greedy for money, but gentle, not quarrelsome, not covetous; one who rules his own house well, having children in submission with all reverence (for if a man does not know how to rule his own house, how will he take care of the house of God?); not a novice, lest being puffed up with pride he fell into the same condemnation as the devil. Moreover he must have a good testimony among those who are outside, lest he fall into reproach and the snare of the devil.*

Have you ever wondered why there is so much trouble, scandal and disgrace in some churches? There have been so many Pastors, Priest, and Bishops accused of sexual immorality it makes the head spin. One of the main reasons is most churches do not go by the guidelines God has set for her.

When we look at how the Church operated successfully in the first century, we find the elders' only job was to go to God for the people and go to the people for God. The Elders would rule the Church through prayer and obedience to His Word.

First of all, God tells us those who want to be Bishop/Pastor/Elder desire a good work. God informs us Bishops/Pastors/Elders must be blameless; they should not be practicing sin. The only way to be blameless is to be in Christ Jesus our Lord; it is abiding in Jesus and Jesus abiding in the leaders of the Church. More so, the Bishop/Pastor/Elder's must have the heart of Jesus and live in the Fruit of the Spirit continuously. To be blameless takes maturity, it takes the practice of perfection to hone, refine, groom, and polish the Fruit of the Spirit properly.

The Bishops/Pastors/Elders should have only one wife, or be a one woman kind of man. It should not be in the Church leader's spirit to be wife/husband shopping inside the Church or out. When a Church leader entertains bedding down women other than his wife, then he is diluting the power of the Holy Spirit within him. There are too many Bishops/Pastors/Elders' that are divorcing their spouses and remarrying their secretaries, worship leaders, or anything else with a short skirt and a smile. A little leaven leavens the whole body and when the leader of the Church is involved with these dark activities, the Church will suffer and will be subject to all evil the enemy sends their way. The Bible tells us the judgment of preachers and teachers (leaders) will be much stricter than everyone else.

Bishops/Pastors/Elders must be temperate, moderate, pleasant, comfortable, and practice self-control. Leaders are supposed to be sober-minded, not wishy-washy or unstable in their thinking, or the Scriptures. Leaders should not be power hungry but should be meek which is defined as power under control. Going on tangents is not a fruit of the Spirit for leaders. They must have good behavior and are hospitable, friendly, generous, cordial, and sociable. Bishops/Pastors/Elders must have the ability to teach and able to break down the Scriptures and have the ability to define their meaning. As God worked through Jesus, the Holy Spirit should work through the leaders.

Leaders of the Church should not be given to wine. The Greek word for 'given' is prŏsĕchō and is defined as, "to hold the mind," "pay attention to," "be cautious about," "apply one to," and "adhere to." So leaders should not let wine hold your mind, making intoxicated decisions are bad enough in the world, but in the pulpit it is a disaster. A mind on marijuana cannot make a sober decision as well as cocaine, heroin, acid, uppers and downers, or even heavy use of prescription drugs. If we are to be drunk, we should be drunk in the Holy Spirit where we pray and praise until the wonderful aura of the Holy Ghost becomes heavy, delightful and overwhelming.

As leaders, we are not to be violent, for violence is the opposite of love. If a Bishop/Pastor/Elder is greedy for money, then trouble is on the horizon for the love of money is the root of all evil. Leaders of the Church should be gentle and not quarrelsome, nor covetous. Leaders of the Church should be happy with whatever God gives them.

Bishop/Pastor/Elders should rule their personal house well. The house of the local leader of the Church should be a house of love and peace and order. His children should be well-behaved and godly. If the children are not well-behaved and godly but were brought up in the ways of the Lord, it shouldn't be held against the leader. [See *Proverbs 22:6*] God tells us that if the Bishop/Pastor/Elder cannot run their own house, they will not be successful in operating the house of God. If the leaders' personal lives are in shambles, then the Church will be in shambles. There is an old saying, as the leader goes, so does the Church.

The Bible tells us leaders need to have some experience in being a Christian; they should not be a novice, or a beginner, trainee, rookie, or even a greenhorn. The Greek word for elder is presbuteros and it means "aged." Every new believer should spend time with the Word of God and study God, Jesus and the Holy Spirit and their identity of who he/she is in Christ Jesus. Novices need to soak in the Word for years to get an understanding of their covenant, their relationship with God and Jesus, and listening to the Holy Spirit. They need to get to the point where the Word is strong in them and there is evidence of salvation in their lives. Whenever a novice receives a high-ranking position in Church, there is a very good chance that pride will find its way in the heart of the young person and corrupt him. Power corrupts, and absolute power corrupts absolutely. I've never seen a natural baby run their household, and a babe in Christ cannot be an effective leader in the house of God.

There are some Bishops/Pastors/Teachers who are hirelings. Jesus talks about them in *The Gospel of John 10:12*. Hirelings really don't care for the flock, but they do care about the offerings from the flock. They are stand up Christians in the good times, but when things get tight, they will leave. They love the prestige of the title of Pastor, Bishop, Apostle or whatever fits their fancy in that season, but they don't have the Spiritual sense to act according. They love the idea of ruling over a flock simply for what they can get out of the flock. Hirelings cannot fulfill the Scripture in *1 Timothy*, nor would they care to.

Bishop/Pastor/Elders should have a good reputation with those outside the body of Christ. Those outside the Church know who the Christians are, for they watch and observe them almost daily. They may not go to the Church, but when trouble comes, they will go to the one that has evidence of salvation. They will go to a Christian to go to God on their behalf because they have been watching your life.

Jesus tells us to shepherd the flock, to feed the flock. The shepherd should only speak the Word of God in its purity, in its truthfulness, without veering or deviating to the left or the right.

Every church should use *1 Timothy 3* and *Titus 2* as guidelines for their leaders if they want a true and healthy Church. Just as a car with bad spark plugs doesn't allow the car to run smoothly, Bishop/Pastor/Elders that do not live by the guidelines will run a church into the ground. There should be peace, love, and the power of God working in each church, and it all starts with the leaders.

Prayer

Most gracious Heavenly Father, I bow my knees to You, God and Father of my Lord and Savior Jesus Christ, from Whom the whole family in Heaven and on earth is named, that You would grant me, according to the riches of Your glory, that I may be strengthened with might through Your Spirit in my inner man, so that Christ may dwell in my heart through faith; and that I am being rooted and grounded in love, so that I may be able to comprehend with all the saints, what is the width and length and depth and height – and to know the love of Christ which passes all understanding and knowledge; so that I may be filled with all the fullness of God.

Father, I know that you are able to do exceedingly, abundantly above all that I can ask or think, according to the power that works in me, I give You all the praise and glory and honor through the King of kings and the Lord of lords Christ Jesus for all You have done in my life.

Amen.

Notes:

Notes:

Chapter 18

A Little Leaven *(Part 1)*

Leaven

Matthew 13:33
Another parable He spoke to them: "The kingdom of heaven is like leaven, which a woman took and hid in three measures of meal till it was all leavened."

and...

Matthew 13:33 NIV
The kingdom of heaven is like yeast that a woman took and mixed into a large amount of flour until it worked all through the dough.

In this illustration, God depicts a woman using yeast to make bread. The woman in the natural will mix the yeast in the dough until the yeast is permeated throughout the dough. When yeast is kneaded into dough, it expands by itself. In the spiritual realm, the seed that was sown in your heart will grow, like the yeast in the dough, as you work the Word of God in your life the Kingdom will expand. When you practice the Kingdom dynamics of God, like yeast working in the bread, the power, personality and the wisdom of God will be made manifest in your life. So when a person is born-again, the Holy Spirit works from the inside out as yeast works from the inside out. Instead of the Kingdom of God growing outwardly, it grows by internally. It is the Holy Spirit that does the work.

Leaven represents influence. Influence is the effect of something on a person, thing or event. It is the power someone has to affect other people's thinking or actions by means of argument, example, or the force of personality. It is also the power that comes from wealth, social status or position. Leaven spreads an idea by a proclamation, preaching or teaching a system or doctrine to others, (to those who are uninformed). Leaven can be used to spread either good influence or bad influence. There is the leaven of the Kingdom of God, in which the Good News of salvation is preached and the results of the power of the Word of God. Then there is other leaven, which is bad guidance that will build you up to such a state you don't need God, because you have basically made yourself your own god.

There is a leaven that is not the Word of God. Leaven can also represent evil; this leaven spreads false teaching throughout the world and eventually the Church, until it has more tares than wheat. As yeast spreads throughout the dough, a little bit of leaven, (like corruption), has the ability to corrupt a whole system, the whole Church body. Generally in the Bible, a woman will represent idolatry. [See *Revelations 17*] However in *Matthew 10*, the woman does not represents evil, she represents a Kingdom dynamic.

The leaven of the Kingdom of God produces salvation, healing, deliverance, prosperity, peace, comfort, a sound mind and so on. But the leaven of darkness produces doubt, unbelief, fear, anxiety, selfishness, error and ultimately hell and the Lake of Fire.

In the above parable the three measures of meal is the world. And the woman working the yeast, which is in this case, the influence of Jesus Christ until the doctrine of the Kingdom is manifest or known to the entire world. This will happen at His just before His second coming, after the last Gentile accepts Christ as Lord and Savior. Then the whole world will know He is the King of kings and the Lord of lords and every knee will bow and every tongue will confess that He is Lord

There are different types of leaven in the New Testament. There is the leaven of Heaven, the leaven of Satan, the leaven of the Pharisees, and the leaven of the Sadducees, and the leaven of Herod. We have briefly talked about the Kingdom of Heaven. Now we will move on to the next one.

We witness the practice of spreading leaven, or influence, every day. Its purpose is to sway our lives and train us in whosoever's line of reasoning. On television, on billboards, on the internet and in other forms of social media we see through advertising where thousands of companies try to influence you to buy their products. Car dealerships, restaurants, food chains and food products, clothing, sex enhancement products, beautifying products, body building programs, cooking shows, loan companies, amusement parks, lawyers, self-help programs and many, many other strategies that are promulgated to influence you to partake in their product or business. There are also programs that attempt to influence our ways of thinking, and ways of living. These men and women attempt to guide you to follow their line of thinking through opinions, politics, and laws to determine what's cool and what's not, what is acceptable and what is not acceptable.

The leaven of the Church today should be influencing its congregation through the Word of God by the Holy Spirit. The foundation of every church's doctrine should be the based on Jesus Christ. It should be based on His teaching on Kingdom principles, our ways of thinking, our ways of living and our ways of worshipping the Father. As I said in an earlier chapter, if Jesus is not the foundation or the center of our lives, we are in a cult. The leaven of the doctrine of the Kingdom of God will spread throughout the world until the last person gives their life to Christ. So the Church should always influence the lost to become children of God. The Church should always encourage the children of God to yield to the work of the Holy Spirit until our spirits are leavened with the nature of God.

One day Peter was in Joppa meditating on the roof of Simon the tanner's house and he fell into a trance. God was illustrating a work He would have Peter to do. At the door of the house, there was a delegation from the house of Cornelius who wanted Peter to come to his home in the town of Caesarea to share the Gospel with them. Peter went to Caesarea and shared the Gospel with Cornelius and his whole family was saved. There is power in the rhema (spoken) Word and in this story the leaven or the influence that changed their lives was the testimony of Jesus Christ:

Acts 10:38
How God anointed Jesus of Nazareth with the Holy Spirit and with power, who went about doing good and healing all who were oppressed by the devil.

Our leaven is the testimony of Jesus Christ. The Good News of Him laying down His power and coming to earth as a man to redeem mankind, dying for our sins and delivering us from the kingdom of darkness. Like the woman who spread three measures of meal until it was all leavened, the testimony of Christ spread throughout the house of Cornelius until his entire house was saved. A similar story happened in *Acts 16*, when Paul was beaten and placed in jail for delivering a girl who was practicing demonic activities. While he was in jail, he and Silas praised the Lord and the jail shook, causing all the doors of the jailhouse to open. When the jailer felt the earthquake and saw all the cell doors opened, he assumed all the prisoners had escaped. The jailer was in charge of the prisoners, and if one prisoner escaped, the jailer would have to finish the escaped convict's sentence. If the prisoner had the death penalty, the jailer would have to take that penalty of death because it was the law of the land. So the jailer drew a sword to kill himself but Paul stopped him with the news that no prisoner escaped. This opened the door for Paul to witness the love and power of Christ Jesus and the end result was that the jailer and his entire household were saved.

The influence of the doctrine of Christ has saved millions of people from the kingdom of darkness with eternal separation from God and placed them into the Kingdom of Light and in the eternal presence of the Lord. The seed (the Word of God) of the Kingdom blossomed into faith when it was watered with the spoken Word. Spoken and heard! As the Word of God speaks, faith is produced and causes changes in our lives and circumstances to give us a renewed life. Faith comes by hearing and hearing by the Word of God. *Romans 10:17*. Our faith in God is what changes us and also our faith in Him pleases God. *Hebrews 11:6*. The Bible says that God is a rewarder of those who diligently seek Him.

Notes:

Notes:

Chapter 19

A Little Leaven *(Part 2)*

Beware of the Leaven of the Pharisees

The leaven of the Pharisees is a religious system in which the concept of God is very important to them. However, the relationship with God is not important and God is actually treated as a distant relative. Their relationship with God is like your relationship with your sixth cousin on your stepparent's side of the family who live three thousand miles away. A close relationship is not there. The Pharisees pray to be seen by men and put on airs when they fast to seem important and godly to the casual eye.

The leaven of the Pharisees embraces God in theory but they do not practice what God teaches. In fact, this type of leaven holds the grand theory of God but at the same time, it makes its own rules. These rules are generally allocated to allow them to live comfortably as leaders but it often causes a burden on the poor and uneducated men and women. This is because this leaven is not giving Words of life; they are just words of tradition and religiosity.

Another attribute of the leaven of the Pharisees is the form of godliness but without the power of God. They claim to be someone important without any evidence of being important (other than their fine clothing). It is like claiming to be rich without a dime in your pocket. Your confession and your life are not one and the same.

2 Timothy 3:5
Having the form of godliness but denying its power. And from such people turn away.

Those having the form of godliness today are the preachers or ministers that put on spiritual airs of importance. They dress exclusively and live lavishly but their works are moot and superficial and consist of superficial meetings, dinners and programs that do not have an effect on the lost people who came to get help in spiritual matters. When a lost person goes into one of these services, they will come out just as lost as they were when they went in. When prayer is performed in these meetings, there is practically no change because even though this leaven insists in praying, they do not believe in an active God and they don't believe you will get an answer to your prayers. Instead, they will give you emotional entertainment that will fire you up through theatrical mannerisms in order to preach to you what you want to hear. This is a form of godliness.

One of the problems in some of today's churches is that, "The cross is not preached!" When the cross is not preached, there is not a solid foundation for a changed life. When a person does not understand that Jesus died for our sins, then that person will not have a righteous conscience and will not come into the knowledge of the fact that through the cross, we have become the righteousness of God in Christ Jesus. This person will not come to the knowledge that by the stripes that He took on our behalf, we are healed. He will not know Jesus as a deliverer. He will not know Jesus as a provider, a mediator, an advocate and friend. And certainly, the person cannot be born-again unless he goes though the cross. So when the cross is denied, the works of the Holy Spirit will not be active in your life. It is a dangerous thing to deny any part of the mission of Jesus Christ. It's like saying I want God but I don't believe in that Jesus fella. Practicing Christianity without Christ being involved is *having a form of godliness but denying the power thereof.*

When Jesus is not preached, when the light of the Word is not proclaimed so that it exposes the darkness, then the darkness has the ability to remain steadfast in the position he has established and things will remain at status quo. No growth, no change, everything will stay as it is.

Spiritual Warfare and The Church

Galatians 5:9
A little leaven leavens the whole lump.

Paul said be sure that you keep yourselves away from all evil. Make sure the Word of God is strong in you because a little leaven, a little false doctrine, a little spirit of error will leaven (will saturate) your whole being, your life. This means a little dirt can ruin you. A little bit of flesh pleasing doctrine, a little sin, and crooked misdirected deeds if gone unchecked can plunge a person into full-fledged darkness and sin.

An example of this is, when a person looks at a little pornography. He is opening the door for sexual immorality, which is demonic. A little leaven is that first look. When that first look is lingered upon, demonic spirits will begin titillating you to take further action. Imaginations of sexual liaisons will pop up in your brain like they do on your computer. When your imaginations have run its course, it will bloom into obsessions. This action will lead you into looking for someone to satisfy the lust you have been demonically renewing your mind. This leads people to clubs, strip joints, laundry mats, grocery stores, red light districts, and day care centers to satisfy their urge for sexual contact. For some, they will hide in the bushes so that they may jump out and take what they want. Porn (lust of the flesh) has its hooks in so many people that sexual predators are being televised as entertainment. Sin will take you further than you want to go and keep you longer than you want to stay. Small activities will always have the propensity to grow up into huge events.

James 1:14-15
But each one is tempted when he is drawn away by his own desires and enticed. Then, when desire has conceived, it gives birth to sin; and sin, when sin is full grown, brings forth death.

Another example is smoking marijuana. Many people believe this is a harmless herb and it is easy to control. However, there are countless millions of people who enjoy the high for a period of

197

time and use it as a form of escape only to find out that there is no escape. Others love the herb because the colors of their environment become extremely vigorous and intense. Smokers find their flesh becomes nimble and care-free and caution becomes a bottom feeder on the priority list. However, after a while, the herb does not feed the flesh as it did at the beginning. A need to get back to that euphoric state of being requires stronger and more powerful drugs such as cocaine, heroin, quaaludes, meth, trash, or any and every other drug. The next thing you know, years have passed away, your teeth are rotted, your body is gaunt and emaciated, and there is a high probably you have contracted a virus or two. Your relationship with your family is hindered or destroyed and depression becomes a way of life. A little leaven will open doors and take you to places you never dreamed of, which is a nightmare you can't escape from.

> *Matthew 16:1-4*
> *Then the Pharisees and the Sadducees came, and testing Him asked that He would show them a sign from heaven. He answered and said to them, "When it is evening you say, 'It will be fair weather, for the sky is red'; and in the morning, "It will be foul weather today, for the sky is red and threatening.' Hypocrites! You know how to discern the face of the sky, but you cannot discern the signs of the times. A wicked and adulterous generation seek after a sign, and no sign shall be given to it except the sign of the prophet Jonah."*

This is an interesting conversation between Jesus with the Pharisees and Sadducees. The religious sect had just witnessed the feeding of the four thousand, however, they had eyes to see but they could not perceive what had just happened. I believe their hearts were so harden against the Son of Man that whatever He did, they would find fault, or misinterpret what they witnessed. The sign of darkness was strong in them.

They asked Jesus for a sign when they had just witnessed a great sign or miracle. The religious sects were conversant or educated in

Jewish history and may have been looking for fire from the sky as in the days of Elijah. They may have been looking for the sun to stand still as in the days of Joshua. They could have been looking for fire and brimstone to fall from Heaven. Whatever they were looking for, they asked Jesus to perform a sign as if He was performing circus acts. But Jesus rebuked them by calling them hypocrites because their expertise was of the things of the earth and not spiritual things. Jesus was fulfilling Scripture in their presence every day and they could not recognize His works were ordained by God. People of God should recognize the works of God. Nicodemus recognized the works of God. The blind man in *John 9* recognized the works of God. One of the Roman guards recognized Him as the Son of God. Then there are thousands of people that He healed of sickness, disease, leprosy, and demonic possession witnessed the power of God.

Jesus told them, *"As Jonah was in the belly of a big fish for three days, the Son of God would be in the earth for three days."* (Paraphrased.) That was the sign of Jonah, and Jesus would fulfill that also from the Cross of Calvary to the Resurrection Sunday.

Now when the disciples had come to the other side, they had forgotten to take bread. Then Jesus said to them, "Take heed and beware of the leaven of the Pharisees, and the Sadducees."

Today, we need to watch out, be aware, and be mindful not to stray away from the Gospel of Christ Jesus our Lord. Statements like, "I don't know," or "I don't think" is the little leaven but when pondered on or mused, it can grow into unbelief and doubt and will wreck your walk and usher you into the realm of hypocrites. We must make sure we are true and pure in our worship, our relationship and our walk to God.

Notes:

Chapter 20
A Little Leaven *(Part 3)*

The Leaven of Herod

Mark 8:15
Then He charged them, saying, "Take heed, beware of the leaven of the Pharisees and the leaven of Herod."

The leaven of Herod is different than the leaven of the Pharisees. This type of leaven is basically an anti-God/anti-Christ leaven. Its influence is atheistic at best and its emphasis is based in man. Its strength is man based systems born in the minds of carnal men and its motto is 'God helps those who help themselves.' It is ironic that the system is an anti-God system but believes that God helps those who help themselves. This leaven is also spawned from the kingdom of darkness. The kingdom of darkness is one of confusion, willful blindness, ignorance, and error.

The influence of Herod is one of a self-made deity while being atheistic in nature. This leaven believes that you are the answer to your own problem because you are a self-made god/man. This 'take responsibility for yourself,' doctrine is a wonderful idea in the eyes of the world. However, man cannot save himself.

Also included in the realm of leaven is politics. However, politics has always been a game of status, position, prominence, and prestige in the clutches of the dark kingdom. Most political governments do not even use the Kingdom of God principles as an example for governing the people of the land.

For instance, man is imperfect. So when men are in charge of the government then the system will also be imperfect. Man has a

201

tendency to run the business of the country by his wisdom or the wisdom of his peers, councils, cabinets, legislatures, senates and so on. When men get into position to run something, most of the time God and His ways are edged out.

It is the same way in a lot of churches around the world. In most churches, one board or another operates the church, or makes decisions or influence the church with their own personal leaven. However, the Bible clearly says that Jesus is the head of the Church and all direction should be taken from Him. The Pastor is not even the head of the Church, the Pastor of each church should be taking direction from the Holy Spirit and executed in that fashion.

When my flesh is involved, then I am not doing my church any earthly good. But when Christ is followed and obeyed, then the light of Christ will be evident to all in the Church. There must be evidence of the Church living in the light. It is not the numbers so many people think as evidence of salvation; it is the spiritual condition of the Church that is obedient to the Word of God that will be the evidence of salvation.

The Leaven of Satan

2 Timothy 3:1-5a

But know this, that in the last days perilous times will come: For men will be lovers of themselves, lovers of money, boasters, proud, blasphemers, disobedient to parents, unthankful, unholy, unloving, unforgiving, slanderers, without self-control, brutal, despisers of good, traitors, headstrong, haughty, lovers of pleasure rather than lovers of God, having a form of godliness but denying its power.

Today, we can see the leaven or the influence of Satan almost everywhere we look, and he is the author of the leaven of the Pharisees and Herod. Like the good woman who took and hid the three measures of meal till it was all leavened, The Prince of the Power of the Air is injecting an abundance of rotten yeast into the world, influencing the world with his antichrist system.

202

Since he already has the world in his unholy hands, he works in the churches throughout the world. He starts at the top of the religious food chain as he did with the elders in *Ezekiel 8*. If he can influence the leaders with his doctrine, then he knows they will influence their followers. As he did with the leaders of all the cults, he also does with Bishops, Pastors and all other leaders in the Church if he can.

He is spreading the leaven of sexual immorality through several churches around the world. This leaven was active in the cities of Sodom and Gomorrah which God destroyed. It was active in *Judges 19* in the story of a man and his concubine in Ephraim, in which the tribe of Benjamin went to war against Israel. This leaven flourished in the Greek culture and also in the Roman Empire where their gods, (demons) were very active in same sex activities. Today, there are many churches that adhere to this doctrine of demons. Also there are many churches that are splitting because some believe that God is fine with it while others disagree and believe what God says about the subject. This strong and powerful spirit has caused many clergy including Bishops, Pastors, and other officers of the Church to engage in sexual immorality with women, men and children in the Name of Jesus. This leaven has spread throughout the world and is becoming a normal activity in the eyes of the unsaved. Unsaved preachers and teachers in some churches really believe that God has changed His mind about sexual immorality.

The Bible says that Satan will try to change laws in the last days, and the Church in this era is a witness. It would be useless for the Church to fight this activity because God said this would happen. We do not want to fight against God. What He says will happen. The best thing for the Church that serves the True and Living God to do is to continue to be a witness of the lifesaving changes that comes in Christ Jesus. We are not called to picket or protest the courts, because that involves the flesh however, we are to speak what God has to say about any given subject and let the Holy Spirit do His work. The Church operates from a position of strength, and we are not to be a part of religious lynch mobs operating in the guise of Christianity.

Notes:

Chapter 21

Lining-up with God's Word

Renewing Our Minds

We are in a world that's focused on bringing every living soul in line with the world. The world wants us to focus on offenses, current events, the latest fashion, the latest CD/DVD, the latest technology, the latest surgical procedure that would enhance our looks, the latest pill that will allow us to have better sex, the latest car with all the amenities, the latest hamburger that you cannot live without. New products are created or improved every day for people to use and fall in love with to keep their minds focused on vain living. From shoes to fish sandwiches, from swimming pools to new houses, from new phones to new suits, from new cars to the latest fad, people are focused with keeping up with the Joneses. There are some who focus more on the care of animals (even deadly snakes) than on human beings. There are committees, teams, groups, and think tanks that are paid millions of dollars to get your attention so that you may dedicate your life to one cause or another. The world wants every human being on the planet to focus on anything except the Word of God.

Then there are the thousands of religions and cults that want your support, attention and focus. The idea is to present a god that allows you to be yourself, to be free from religion and the strictness of rules and regulations. Some are public with their endeavors while others are private in their activities. The hook they throw is a product, activity, or actions that allows you to practice or exercise an activity in the flesh. The focus is on things that make you feel good and look good.

As a Christian man or woman, we must realize we are in the world and not of the world. So the most important thing we should do each and every day is renew our minds by the Word of God. We must renew our minds by reading our Bible, spending time with the Lord in prayer and praise to God; we should pray the Word of God and sing praises from the Scripture and from our hearts. Renewing our mind is to roll thoughts of Jesus, God, and the Scriptures over and over in our minds until we are saturated with the idea, the character, and the walk of God's plan for our lives.

Singing in the Spirit is very powerful in renewing our minds. The Apostle Paul said he would sing in the Spirit and sing with understanding. I have witnessed this to be a wonderful experience and words cannot adequately express the euphoric, exhilarated, and ecstatic feeling that comes when we spend this type of time with the True and Living God.

In today's busy world, a lot of people do not have the time to spend hours in reading the Word, or in prayer and praise to the Lord. But we need to make the time every day to spend in the Spirit of God. When we take the time to read one paragraph or just one Scripture and meditate, ponder, consider and roll that Scripture over and over in our minds, we are still renewing our minds.

To renew is to reintroduce, refurbish, and return to a subject. In our case, we need to renew our mind to the Word of God. When we renew our minds by the Word of God, we become strong in the Word of God. When we become strong in the Word of God, we become strong in His character, strong in His wisdom, strong in His nature, strong to obedience in His Word. When we are full of the Word, we are living in the will of God.

When we renew our minds, it makes it difficult for the enemy to disrupt our lives for *"Greater is He that is in you than he that is in the world."* Satan cannot touch God and he cannot touch any man/woman of God with any success because the Spirit of God is strong in us.

Our every action begins with a thought, when our thought life lines up with the Word of God, then our actions will line up with the Word of God. When our thoughts, action and lifestyle line up with the Word of God; we will be living in the fruit of the Spirit and will be powerful witnesses for the Lord.

Jesus said, *"Out of the abundance of the heart, the mouth speaks"* When we are full of the Word of God and we get squeezed, tried, or tested by the devil or the trials of life, then the Word of God will come out of our mouths. If we have been renewing our minds with cable television, the news, porn, drugs, or the doctrine of the world, then that will come out of our mouths. What we put in is what will come out.

In the *15th chapter of Matthew*, Jesus corrected the Pharisees and scribes who were complaining against the disciples of Jesus. They believed the disciples were transgressing, or misbehaving, or disobeying the commandments of God, because they did not wash their hands before they ate bread from the temple. The Pharisees believed the disciples were defiling themselves. But Jesus counteracted by telling them they were transgressing the commandments of God because of their traditions. For God says, *'Honor your father and mother,'* and *'he who curses father or mother shall be put to death.'* But the religious sects changed the law by saying whatever we get, we got from God and there is no reason to honor our father and mother. Jesus further told them they made the commandment of God of no effect by the traditions they created and adopted unto themselves. You see, even though they were the upper echelon of the Jewish people, they did not renew their minds according to the Scripture. They renewed their minds according to themselves.

Hypocrites!

Matthew 15:7-9

Hypocrites! Well did Isaiah prophesy about you, saying: These people draw near to Me with their mouth, and honor Me with their lips, but their heart is far from me. In vain they worship Me, teaching as doctrines the commandments of man."

If we do not renew our minds daily, we will find ourselves out of the loop, off base, and before too long, we corrupt the Scriptures just as Satan wants us to. When we don't renew our minds, we become easy targets for Satan because we become 'of the world' through our unrenewed minds.

Jesus told them it is not what goes in your mouth that defiles a man, but what comes out of your mouth – that defiles a man. So it is not what you eat that defiles you, it is what comes out of your mouth that defiles you. For our mouths speaks what is in our hearts, or on our minds. Jesus said,

Matthew 15:19

For out of the heart proceed evil thoughts, murders, adulteries, fornications, thefts, false witness, and blasphemies.

An unrenewed mind is full of thoughts that are against the ideals of God. These characteristics are those of the kingdom of darkness and procured by the flesh. Again, if we do not renew our minds daily, we will agree with the world's way of thinking, the world's philosophy and our relationship with Jesus will wither and die. He will become a mental assent instead of the Living Word. In this condition, we will think our lives are good and we are blessed and we're on our way to Heaven.

When we renew our minds our heart will process thoughts of goodness, kindness, faithfulness, and honoring God. The difference between a renewed mind and an unrenewed mind is far as the east is from the west.

A Living Sacrifice

Romans 12:1

I beseech you therefore, brethren, by the mercies of God, that you present your bodies a living sacrifice, holy, acceptable to God, which is your reasonable service.

The word beseech is defined as 1: to beg for urgently or anxiously. It also means to 2: to request earnestly, to implore. So there is great emphasis on presenting our bodies as a living sacrifice to the Lord. To present our bodies as a living sacrifice to the Lord is to allow ourselves to serve the Lord, to be obedient to the Lord. A dead sacrifice is worth nothing but a one-time deal. A living sacrifice is a daily action of dying to ourselves, or denying ourselves to operate in the flesh and live by the Spirit unto God. It is an attitude of saying, believing, and living the life of, "It's not about me, it's about the True and Living God that works in me."

Jesus is a perfect example of renewing the mind. He would go up into the hills or into the mountains at night to spend time with God in prayer. The Scripture reveals that He would pray all night in most occasions. When He came down from the mountains, and full of the Holy Ghost, He healed people, deliver people and told the crowd, *"It's not Me who does the works; it is the Father who works through Me that does the works."*

Renewing our minds is meditating, contemplating, pondering, musing, and thinking over the Scriptures, rolling them over and over in our minds until it becomes a part of us. This is not an overnight process, it is a lifelong process and as we matriculate through life, God will use what we have learned by the Scriptures to test us with a circumstance or a situation so that we would know we are on the right track in the Kingdom of God. For instance, if I am renewing my mind on loving my brothers as I love myself, then God places me in a situation to actually love my brother. If my mind is renewed, then I will get through the situation in the love of God. Remember, the Scriptures say that our steps are ordered by the Lord. This is God's plan for growth in the Kingdom of God. He places us in situations that will give us a chance to be Christ-like and the only way we can be successful is by a renewed mind.

We must remember, as God ordered the steps of Jesus to cause Him to be victorious in everything He did, He also orders our steps so we may have the same results. And as Jesus gave God the glory, so will His children give Him glory for the works of the Gospel. We must remember it is God working through us to obtain whatever He wants.

> *Romans 6:13*
> *And do not present your members as instruments of unrighteousness to sin, but present yourselves to God as being alive from the dead and your members as instruments of righteousness to God.*

What this means is that we are not to use our hands to steal any longer. We are not to use our hands to violate people, or use them to hold firearms to rob folks any longer. We are not to use our lips to lie on people or to speak words of corruption any longer. We are not to use our lips to speak boastfully on things that do not glorify God any longer. We are not to use our feet to go to dope houses, whore houses, gambling houses, ungodly churches and activities, strip clubs, your neighbor's bed, shady alleys, or any place that does not honor the Lord our God any longer. Remember, a little leaven leavens the whole batch.

As a living sacrifice, we are to use our hands to help people. We are to use our lips to encourage people and speak the Word of God over their lives. God calls this our *reasonable service*, or this is the natural way Christians are supposed to live. As living sacrifices, we are to use the gift God gave us to educate the Church in spiritual matters. We are to proclaim Jesus as Lord. We are to teach His ways and promote His love, truth and deity for all who ask.

Instructors in Righteousness

To be holy and to be sanctified are similar. Both terms are 'to be set apart for the Lord's holy use'. It is God who sanctifies us to preach the Gospel or to teach (explain) the Gospel. It is God who sanctifies us to be a deacon or a praise leader or any of the fivefold ministry Jesus set upon this earth. The Scripture below reads Jesus set apart, or sanctified, some to hold and operate in certain offices for the advancement of the Kingdom of God.

Ephesians 4:11
And He Himself gave some to be apostles, some prophets, some evangelists, and some pastors and teachers, for the equipping of the saints for the work of the ministry, for the edifying of the body of Christ, till we all come to the unity of the faith and of the knowledge of the Son of God, to a perfect man, to the measure of the stature of the fullness of Christ.

Apostles, Prophets, Evangelists, Pastors and Teachers are to build up the children of God with the Word of truth in humility, or absent of pride. God gives these men and women the grace, (His divine influence or ability) to teach the saints, equip the saints to live a holy lifestyle and for the work of the ministry. God gives these men and women the grace, (His divine influence or ability) to edify, enlighten, inform, instruct, and educate the people of God until we all come to the unity of the faith and of the knowledge of the Jesus, the Son of God. God gives these men and women the grace, (His divine influence or ability) to bring

211

everyone in the Kingdom of God to perfection or maturity, to the fullness of Christ. This can only be done with renewed minds.

When the Pastor is preaching or a Teacher is teaching the Gospel, minds are being renewed. *Faith comes by hearing and hearing by the Word of God.* The leader of the Church may have to tell a story or teach Spiritual truths more than one time before the congregation understands these truths – but as the congregation listens to the Word over and over and ponder over what the leader said – that is also renewing our minds.

Overcoming Temptation

Romans 12:2
And do not be conformed to this world, but be trans-formed by the renewing of your mind, that you may prove what is that good and acceptable and perfect will of God.

Renewing our minds is allowing the Word of God to take residence in our thought life. To conform means 'to mold' or 'to form.' Instead of being molded, shaped and precast by the values of this world, or Satan, we apply ourselves to renew our minds according to the Word of God. Thoughts dedicated to the world and its trepidations will produce a life that is not stable and the mind will be tossed to and fro and tuned to the current events of the world. But the mind that is dedicated to the Kingdom of God will stand in truth and will be able to stand in times trouble. When we do this, we are able to resist the wiles of the devil and control our flesh because we have habitually meditated on God's truth. This will allow the Holy Ghost to mold, guide and escort our lives into victorious living. Our thoughts and behavior will have a guard on them as we go through life.

The more we read by the Spirit of God, the more we control the thoughts that come to our heads. When we read the Word of God, that Word washes and cleanses our thoughts. The Word strengthens our thought process as we develop the mind of Christ.

We cannot stop evil thoughts that come to our minds, but we can control them. I like what Brother Kenneth E. Hagin said years ago, *"We can't stop birds from flying over our heads, but we can stop them from making a nest in our hair."* We can't stop thoughts from coming but we certainly have the ability not to dwell on the trespassing thoughts. When thoughts come that are outside the realm of God's goodness, or ways, or the doctrine of Christ, we should take that thought captive by falling back on what God says.

For example, when a beautiful woman or a handsome man walk across your path, the flesh may want to have sex with them, but a renewed mind will reject the thoughts because it does not bear witness of the covenant of Christ. If the mind is not renewed, then the flesh will try to dominate situation and before you know it you're knee deep in fornication or adultery.

I heard a Minister several years ago teaching on the subject of taking our thoughts captive. She pointed out that when a thought is not of God comes to us; we should get ten Scriptures that talk about the thoughts that are trying to plague us. For instance, when we are bombarded with lustful thoughts, we should look up ten Scriptures that reveal God's opinion about lust and how to combat it. As we read those ten Scriptures and say them out loud, we will find that the invading thoughts had vanished. As we answer attacks from the enemy with the Word of God we should also put the Word of God on thoughts that are contrary to His Word. That is what Jesus did to the Devil in *Matthew 4*. And that will be what will happen when we apply the Word of God to any given situation. The Word of God is Light, and the words of the enemy are darkness; so when the light is revealed or illuminated or uncovered the darkness runs away.

James 1:12-15
Blessed is the man who endures temptation; for when he

213

has been approved, he will receive the crown of life, which the Lord has promised to those who love Him. Let no one say when he is tempted, "I am tempted of God". For God cannot be tempted by evil, nor does He Himself tempt anyone. But each one is tempted when he is drawn away by his own desires and enticed. Then, when desire has conceived, it gives birth to sin; and sin, when it is full-grown, brings forth death.

Temptation comes from all kinds of sources. Temptation could be women or men. It could be drugs or the excessive use of alcohol. It could be gambling or stealing or lying, or gossiping, or just plain ol' cussin' – or just breaking the law of man or the law of God. Temptation is an inner desire to participate in an activity we should not be involved with. Remember we are set apart for holy use. Temptation is a craving to do something right or wrong. We may be tempted to buy an ice cream float, or a rib eye steak. So temptation is not sin in itself, it is what we are tempted with that makes all the difference and what we do with the temptation.

Blessed is the man who endures temptations. We are blessed when we handle our trials with patience and God's counsel. If we do not murmur or complain during the trial but stand on the Word of God; then we are working our covenant and God will be pleased with us. We endure temptation by not letting the temptation affect us. We are successful when we overcome these errant thoughts and dismiss the temptation for what it really is – a pathway or an avenue to sin. So those who remain steadfast under testing will receive the Crown of Life. As Job went through extraordinary circumstances and did not sin, we also can go through problems, situations and circumstances as a Christian should. When we go through these trials, we should praise God, meditate on His Word, stay in prayer and ask for help from the Holy Spirit.

Evil thoughts do not come from God. They come from the

evil one and from your flesh. Evil thoughts operate exclusively in the natural man, and they operate regularly in the carnal Christian. The spiritual man has learned to cast these thoughts away. He has learned when they come to him, he must make a conscious effort to think on something that is good and pure. Evil thoughts will operate in anyone that lets it.

So when evil thoughts come, don't think they are from God. God will not tempt you with sin, He will, however, allow you to be tested for your spiritual growth. These tests are to help you grow so you can know beyond a shadow of a doubt that you believe as the Word says we are to believe.

Declaration
I am born of God and Satan no longer has a hold on me
I am a new creation in Christ Jesus
according to the Scriptures
And have passed from death to life
I am born-again and my old life has passed away,
Now all things have become new.
God's opinion is now my opinion
Because I agree with God
I am now the righteousness of God in Christ Jesus
I can love as God loves
I am strong in the Lord and in the power of His might.
I am the head and not the tail
I am above and not beneath
I can do all things in Christ Who strengthens
I abide in the Word and the Word abides in me
I am One with Christ because He is One with me
I am One with God because He is One with me
I am a dwelling place for the
True and Living God

Notes:

Chapter 22

Strongholds

The Effects of Strongholds *(Part 1)*

The Bible teaches us we tempt ourselves. When we do not renew our minds and allow it to wander, we could very well find ourselves entertaining a lust of the flesh, the lust of the eyes or the pride of life. When we amuse our minds, we become enticed. When we keep thinking in error, it becomes an obsession, and obsessions will turn into strongholds in our minds.

A stronghold is a prison that keeps your thoughts captive. Its thinking is set in stone. For instance Isis, a branch of Islam believes that non-Muslims are infidels or unbelievers and if they die performing their duty in jihad, they would be greeted with 72 big breasted virgins when they get to Heaven. The Southern Christian Church was the home of the KKK hundreds of years ago and they believed they were Christians at that time. They truly believed they were doing the Lord's work. David Koresh influenced the minds of his members into believing he was Jesus Christ. Jim Jones' influence was so strong; people killed themselves drinking Kool-Aid laced with poison. Heaven's Gate was a cult in California that committed mass suicide while waiting for their spaceship hiding behind the moon. These are just a few atrocities of the millions of people who threw their lives away because their minds were unrenewed or unregenerate.

Here is an example of how this works: Homosexuality is a mammoth subject for debate in today's world. (Not in the Bible, in the world) The thought of homosexuality began in the mind of everyone who chose that lifestyle. Every action that is taken in our lives is a result of our thoughts. Satan, the devil, or one of his imps will plant a seed by whispering in the ears of men, "You are not really a man; there is a woman inside of you trying to get out." He would continue with, "God made a mistake when he made you a man because you know in your heart there is a blossoming woman held captive in your body." Scientists say it only takes about 10 seconds for a thought to be planted in a human brain. The subject will be enticed or lured when he meditates on these statements the devil suggested and will begin to rehearse these statements in his natural mind. After a period of time in thinking these thoughts he will become fixated with the idea of being female and begin to practice the mannerisms of women, if he hasn't already. Then once these obsessions become entrenched, fixed, imbedded, his psyche, and deep-rooted in his mind, the man will be out of the closet and impersonating a woman. He will dress like a woman, try to talk like a woman, flirt like a woman and will even go as far as having an operation so that his body and his mind can attempt to be one. Then this person will go find a mate who is also sexually immoral and marry him. This is a stronghold, this person will believe it until death, and the only way to break a stronghold is through the power of Jesus Christ.

Another example of strongholds that plagues our society is school shootings. The Columbine High School Massacre was not the first time children were shot and killed in school. However, it was the first one that received unprecedented coverage from the news media. The earliest known school shooting happened in July 1764 when four Lenape American Indians shot and killed the schoolmaster and ten children.

There is only one author who manipulated these hundreds of school shooting from the 1764 Pontiac Rebellion School Massacre to the shooting on April 11, 2014, at the Detroit East English

Preparatory Academy and beyond – Satan. He uses the same strategy, the power of suggestion upon an unrenewed mind and the results are deadly. Again, it starts with a simple suggestion in the mind of a child who 1. Has no friends or. 2. Is being bullied by others or 3. Is an outcast that cannot fit in with the rest of the students! In most school shootings, the victims are children killing children. Satan plants a thought of dislike, hatred, distaste, and extreme displeasure in the mind of the child that has been bullied or talked about or even rejected by his peers. When his feelings are hurt, the 'enemy of the Trinity' steps in and waters the seeds of disdain into his human spirit, "It is not right! I'm going to even the score! I'm going to kill em! I want revenge!" The child's fragile mind runs several different scenarios through his head until his thoughts are rooted with revenge. Then a plan is put together in his mind when he becomes obsessed with getting even. By the time his obsession is full grown, it elevates into a stronghold in his mind –and then it is time for action. With the help of the Prince of the Power of the Air, the action has taken place and another tragedy is the final outcome.

This three step process is employed, implemented and applied each and every time; imaginations to obsession and obsession to strongholds, and it's the strongholds in the mind of individuals that bring about an action that changes the lives of all involved. Millions of lives have been affected by this process and millions more will be affected if their minds are not renewed in Christ Jesus. Divorces transpire, robberies are enacted, murders and violence are performed, coups, assassinations, setting traps to climb the corporate ladder, stealing your neighbor's wife, kidnapping children and young women as sex slaves, world dictatorship, and all other evils are the results of this three step process he has used from the beginning of time. It is very important for the children of God to renew their minds daily.

The Effects of Strongholds *(Part 2)*

Matthew 15:17-20a

Do you not understand that whatever enters the mouth goes into the stomach and is eliminated? But those things which proceed out of the mouth come from the heart, they defile a man. For out of the heart proceed evil thoughts, murders, adulteries, fornications, thefts, false witness, and blasphemies. These are the things, which defile a man...

We will have trouble with our flesh as long as we live in these dirt suits (our skin). Our flesh will always be enmity against God. Our flesh wants to rule and the Holy Ghost within us needs to teach and guide so it basically comes down to who you feed. If you are constantly feeding on television shows, movies and unwholesome music of the world, swindling people, sexually active outside of marriage, climbing to the top of the corporate ladder by any means necessary, joining a cult, or dwelling on any unpleasant, distasteful, or insalubrious activities, then you will be weak in your spirit and you will fall for anything the devil throws your way. But if you are feeding on the Word of God you will be strong in your spirit. You will be able to see the devil clearly when his game is presented. It is like a man that has two pit bulls; he feeds one and not the other. Over a period of time both dogs are in the same cage and they began to fight. Which one will win? The one that has been fed will win the fight for he will be much stronger than the one that wasn't fed. Christians that do not feed on the Word of God will be pimped, used, abused, extorted, stepped on and defeated by any and every thing that comes down the pike.

When we are not feeding on the Word, our conversation will expose us. Out of the heart will produce the truth of what you have been feeding on. If we have been feeding on violence, then words of violence will proceed out of our mouths. It is the same way with lust. I know a man that let television mold his mind. Every time a well-endowed woman appeared on television commercials selling hamburgers, cars, or what-so-ever, he would make a comment on what he wanted to do with the woman's breast. This line of thinking became a stronghold and landed him in prison with multiple life sentences. Sin will take you further than you want to go and keep you longer than you want to stay. Whatever you focus on, will be the ruler of your life.

Today, the devil works the same tactics he has been polishing from the beginning of time. To create doubt and unbelief is a trademark of the kingdom of darkness. When a child of God receives a Word through another believer, through the Bible, or by revelation knowledge, a thought will eventually try to creep in to nullify the Word he had received. For instance, a believer is sick and he reads:

Isaiah 53:4-5
Surely He has borne our grief's and carried our sorrows; yet we esteem Him stricken, smitten by God, and afflicted. But He was wounded for our transgressions, He was bruised for our iniquities; the chastisement for our peace was upon Him, and by His stripes we are healed.

If he is a believer in Jesus Christ then faith comes. Believers are believers and we believe everything that Jesus did and everything Jesus said. So when we believe the Scriptures, we should believe in the results. *Jesus was wounded for our transgressions, (wrongdoings, disobediences, indiscretions and offenses). He was bruised for our iniquities, (crimes, sins, and vices). The chastisement (rebuke, discipline, and punishment) for our peace was upon Jesus.* So by His stripes we are healed in our spirit and our bodies. Some ministers believe Jesus only healed our spirit, however, He also fulfilled the healing of our bodies according to *Luke 4:18.*

221

Isaiah 61:1

The Spirit of the Lord God is upon Me, because the Lord has anointed Me to preach good tidings to the poor; He has sent Me to heal the brokenhearted, to proclaim liberty to the captives, and the opening of the prison to those who are bound. [See also *Luke 4:18*]

An example of the faithfulness of Jesus is found in *Matthew 4:23-25* when

Jesus went about Galilee, teaching in their synagogues, preaching the Gospel of the Kingdom, and healing all kinds of sicknesses and all kinds of diseases among the people. Then when His fame went throughout Syria; they brought to Him all sick people who were afflicted with various diseases and torments, and those who were demon possessed, epileptics, and paralytics; and He healed them all. Great multitudes followed Him – from Galilee, and Decapolis, Jerusalem, Judea and beyond the Jordan.

I believe every person was made whole when Jesus performed miracles in the area. The people demonstrated great faith by bringing their sick and afflicted, their demon possessed and the tormented, the paralytics and the disenfranchised to the Master and the Master healed them all.

Since Jesus healed those from Galilee, and Decapolis, Jerusalem, Judea and beyond the Jordan, won't He heal you as well? These cities and towns are no different than Oklahoma City, Oklahoma; Dallas, Texas; Tampa Bay, Florida; Chicago, Illinois; London, England; Paris, France; Freetown, Sierra Leone; Hong Kong, China; or Rio De Janeiro, Brazil. His Word is the same and His healing power has no boundaries. This fact of life should be embedded in every Christian so that it becomes a reality for the Christian.

222

Psalms 107:20
He sent His word and healed them all.

A thought will come to you saying, "If this is true, then why are you still sick, or why are you still feeling the symptoms of a condition in your body." There's that word again, "if." This is the same tactic he tried on Jesus, if, if, if. In spiritual; matters, when a thought comes to our minds and the thought begins with the word, "if," then we can be reasonably sure this particular thought came from the devil. We need to know there are facts and there is the truth; the facts present evidence that we are not well, but the truth declares we are healed by the power of God.

So we as Christians have to guard our thought life at all times. Jesus tells us we will be attacked just as He was attacked. But the Good News is we have overcome because Jesus has already overcome. If we do not meditate on the thoughts of God, then we will live a life of evil desires in our hearts.

Prayer

Most gracious heavenly Father, Your Word says if I dwell in Your secret place, then I shall hide under Your shadow. Lord, You are my refuge and my fortress, and only in You I will trust. Lord You have delivered me from the snares of the devil and from the perilous pestilences, virus, plagues, diseases, and pandemics. You have covered me with Your feathers and under Your wings I have taken refuge. Your truth is my shield and my buckler. I am not afraid of the terror by night, nor of the evil by day.

Father, Your protection is wonderful for a thousand may fall at my side and ten thousand at my right hand but it shall not come near me and my family. Only with my eyes shall I look and see the reward of the wicked.

You promised me Father that when I make You my dwell-

ing place and my refuge, no evil will happen to me nor shall any plague come near my house; For You shall give Your angels charge over me to keep me in all my ways. In the hands of Your angels they shall bear me up, lest I dash my foot against a stone. And all the evils of the world, I shall trample under my feet.

Lord You said that because I set my love upon You, You shall deliver me and You will set me on high, because I know Your Name. When I call upon You, You will answer me and will be with me in trouble. You said that You will deliver me and honor me and with long life You will satisfy me and You will show me Your salvation. Thank You Father!

In Jesus Holy and Righteous Name
Amen

Notes:

Chapter 23
The Ministries of the Eleven

Peter

Peter the Rock, or Simon Bar Jonah, became the leader of the Church in Jerusalem. This is the same Peter who was with Christ on the mountain of transfiguration and witnessed Moses and Elijah in conversation with Jesus on the things to come. This is the same Peter whom the Holy Spirit revealed Jesus as the Christ - the Holy Son of God. This is the same Peter who cut Malchus, the high priest's servant's, ear off and later denied he knew Christ three times on the night of Jesus arrest. But on the day of Pentecost, this same Peter stood up and testified to the multitude that Jesus is the Christ. He is the first disciple that held an altar call in which 3,000 people gave their lives to Jesus the Christ.

Peter and John were involved in healing a paralyzed man at the temple gate which caused a ruckus in Jerusalem. However, it was another opportunity for Peter to preach Christ and rebuke the citizens of Jerusalem on their actions in the crucifixion of Christ.

> Acts 3:14-16
> But you denied the Holy One and the Just and asked for a murderer to be granted to you, and killed the Prince of Life, whom God raised from the dead, of which we are witnesses. And His name, through faith in His name, has made this man strong, whom you see and know. Yes, the faith which comes through Him has given him this perfect soundness in the presence of you all.

Peter was involved in the Ananias and Sapphira incident in which the Holy Spirit revealed to him the true intentions of the couple. Ananias and Sapphira wanted the prestige and be held in high esteem in the early Church by lying about their gift to the Church. I want you to note that the Bible says they lied to the Holy Spirit about the amount of money they made versus the amount of money they gave to the Church. We all know they both died that same day.

> *Acts 5:14-16*
> *And the believers were increasingly added to the Lord, multitudes of both men and women, so that they brought the sick out into the streets and laid them on beds and couches, that at least the shadow of Peter passing by might fall on some of the them. Also a multitude gathered from the surrounding cities to Jerusalem, bring the sick people and those who were tormented by unclean spirits, and they were all healed.*

Jesus told us to preach the Gospel and these signs will follow and Peter did just that. We can see the comparison in the works of Peter, and the other Apostles of course, with the works of Jesus. They are strikingly the same, but that's the point; as Christians we're to do the same things Jesus and the disciples did because the same Spirit that abode in them, abides in us.

In 65 AD, Peter was captured and was sentenced to death in Rome. He told them he was not worthy to be crucified like the Lord Jesus Christ, so the Roman government crucified him upside down.

James *(son of Zebedee)*

Around the year 44 AD, James, the son of Zebedee, was arrested under the authority of King Herod Agrippa who was try-

226

ing to stop the spread of Christianity. He wanted the worship for himself. James' strength in the Lord was so strong it changed the life of his accuser. While on the way to the execution room, James led his accuser to the Lord. The accuser apologized for what he had done and was beheaded with James that day. He was the first Apostle, who had walked with Jesus in His earthly ministry to be executed for the Word of Jesus.

Matthew

Matthew wrote his Gospel in Jerusalem. Jesus commanded the disciples to spread the Gospel starting at Jerusalem and Judea to Samaria and to the utter most parts of the world. When they drew the lots, to see where they would go, Matthew drew Ethiopia.

In Ethiopia, King Aeglipus liked Matthew and highly favored him as he taught and preached and many miracles happen through him. However, when the king died and heathens procured the throne, and Matthew was nailed to the ground with spikes and beheaded in 66 AD.

Jude

Thaddeus, also known as, Jude wrote an epistle bearing his name. He was the younger brother of James the lesser and the half-brother of the Lord Jesus Christ. He traveled to Mesopotamia, Syria, Arabia, and modern day Iran. He preached against idol worship and heathen sacrifices. When the high priest saw they were losing a lot of money and many followers, they attacked Jude and beat him to death in 68 AD.

Simon the Zealot

Simon the Zealot preached in Egypt, North Africa, Mauritania and the Isles of Great Britain. Some say he was crucified in Great Britain in 70 AD, others say he was tortured to death by a Syrian governor. No one knows for sure.

James *(the Just)*

James had been a Bishop in Jerusalem for thirty years. During his time there he wrote *The Epistle of James* as he preached Jesus the Christ, the Holy Son of God, and he converted many to Christ. He spent so much time on his knees they were callused and resembled the knees of a camel. The people nicknamed him James the Just.

One day the Chief High Priest, Scribes, and Pharisees took him to the highest point of the Temple and told him to denounce Jesus as the Christ. But James would not do it, so they pushed him off the steeple to the ground. While on the ground, the people began stoning him because only his legs were broken. While being stoned, he kneeled on his broken legs and prayed for the people who were killing him. One of the priests heard the prayer and tried to stop the stoning, saying, "He is praying for us." But a man hit him in the head with a large piece of lumber and killed James while he was in prayer. This happened around AD 63.

Andrew

One day in Greece around 66 AD, Andrew, the brother of Peter, stood before the governor and defended the Gospel of Jesus Christ. The King asked him, "Are you the one who overthrew the temple of the gods and persuaded men to be a Christian when Rome has abolished this religion?"

Andrew answered that Rome does not understand the truth, and he witnessed to the king and told the king he was not afraid of death. So the king sentenced him to be crucified. While Andrew was hanging on the cross, he continued to be a witness for Christ Jesus. He hung for three days and encouraged those who were nearby to keep with the doctrine of Christ so they could receive eternal life.

After three days, the Christians asked the governor to take

him down from the cross but Andrew did not want to come down and dwell among men so he committed his spirit to the Lord as Jesus did when He was on the cross.

Bartholomew

Bartholomew preached the Gospel for thirty-seven years in Turkey and India. He translated *The Gospel of Matthew* in the Indian language and taught them in their native tongue. In 70 AD, he later went to Armenia where many turned from idolatry to worship Jesus as the Son of God. He also converted the King's brother and his family.

The king told Bartholomew he was unsettling the worship of the gods. He said this because the king's brother gave his life to Christ. Bartholomew answered, *"I have preached the true worship of God throughout your country. I have not perverted your brother and his family, but rather converted them to the truth."*

King Astyages threatened Bartholomew, "Unless you stop preaching Christ and make sacrifices to the god of Ashtaroth, you will be put to death."

Bartholomew answered, *"I would rather seal my testimony with my blood than to do the smallest act against my faith or conscience. I will never sacrifice to your idol."*

The king ordered Bartholomew to suffer so he was beat with rods, and they hung him upside down and skinned him alive. But Bartholomew exhorted the people to believe in Jesus and worship God. The authorities eventually cut off his head just to shut him up to stop him from preaching the Gospel.

Thomas

Thomas the Twin, the disciple who doubted Christ's resurrection, *"I will believe it when I see him,"* traveled throughout the known world preaching the Gospel. His lot fell on India and North Africa. He dreaded living among the savages but God strengthened him and he was able to convert many to Christ.

In 70 AD, he went to Calamina, India where the people worshipped the sun god. Thomas destroyed the image of the god and put a stop to their idolatry through the power of God,

The priests of the fake gods were angry and accused him before their king. The king sentenced him to be tortured with red-hot plates, after that they threw him into a large glowing furnace. Thomas did not feel the heat, or the flames in the furnace and when the priest saw this, they threw spears and javelins at him until one pierced his side and Thomas fell over and died.

Philip

There seems to be two Philips in the New Testament. There seems to be one in the Gospels and one in *The Book of Acts*. There is a Philip that Jesus chose as His disciple in *Matthew 10:3, Mark 3:18, Luke 6:14* and in *John 1:43* we see Philip interacting with Nathaniel. It is certain Jesus chose a man named Philip to be one the twelve. We also find the same Philip in *John 14* saying to Jesus, *"Show us the Father, and it is sufficient for us."*

In *The Book of Acts*, there is a man named Philip who was chosen as one of the seven Deacons.

Acts 6:1-5

"Now in those days, when the numbers of the disciples were multiplying, there arose a complaint against the Hebrews by the Hellenist because their widows were neglected in the daily distribution. Then the twelve summoned the multitude of the disciples and said, "It is not desirable that we should leave the word of God and serve tables. Therefore, brethren seek out from among you seven men of good reputation, full of the Holy Spirit and wisdom, whom we may appoint over this business; but we will give ourselves

to prayer and to the ministry of the word." And the saying pleased the whole multitude. And they chose Stephen, a man full of faith and the Holy Spirit, and Philip..."

The Philip in the Gospels was one of the original twelve disciples; the twelve in this passage (which would include the Philip of the Gospels), chose seven men who were full of the Holy Spirit and wisdom to serve the Church while the original twelve continued in the Word and prayer. Among the seven they chose another man named Philip.

The next time we see Philip is in chapter 8 when he left Jerusalem and preached the Word in Samaria and many signs and wonders followed in the revival. The word got back to the Apostles (The original eleven disciples), in *verse 14* that a powerful revival was occurring in Samaria and they sent Peter and John to verify.

Philip also was involved in sowing a seed into an Ethiopian Eunuch who went back to Ethiopia with the Good News of Jesus as the Christ and started a Church there that still stands today.

In *Acts 21:8,* we find Philip again, this time he is called the Evangelist and one of the seven. He had four virgin daughters who prophesied about Paul in Jerusalem.

Later, he went to Turkey and Syria and he planted many churches there. Idol worship was very strong in Hierapolis and Phrygia and they would not listen to the Gospel of Christ even though he did many miracles there. It is reported he was tied to a pillar and stoned to death around 51 AD.

John

John the Beloved, the Apostle of Christ was the only Apostle to die of natural causes. John was a fisherman, the son of Zebedee and younger brother of James. The two were called sons of Thunder and they left their business and their father when Jesus called them.

John was part of the inner circle with his brother James and Peter. The three disciples were blessed to witness events the other nine disciples were not privileged to witness. At the Mount of Transfiguration, John, his brother and Peter witnessed the face of Jesus shinning like the sun and His clothes were whiter than white. John, his brother and Peter witnessed Moses and Elijah talking with Jesus about things to come. Peter, James, and John also witnessed numerous healings as members of Jesus inner circle. John is known as the disciple who laid his head on the bosom of Jesus.

John was the only Apostle at the trial and the crucifixion of Jesus on the cross. It was there Jesus commissioned him to His mother and to His mother a son. Peter and John both ran to the empty tomb when the women told them Jesus has risen from the dead.

After the Day of Pentecost, when the Holy Spirit engulfed the one-hundred-twenty people that prayed and fasted in the Upper Room since the ascension of Jesus, their ministries took root and took off.

John and Peter were the ones who allowed the Holy Spirit to heal a man and the Gate called Beautiful. They were told to stop preaching Christ but they did it anyway. They were beaten for preaching the Way, the Truth and the Life and they praised the Lord for it.

The Roman Emperor Domitian wanted to kill the beloved Apostle, the Romans tried to poison John but it didn't work. Jesus told them that if they drank any deadly thing – they would not be harmed. The evil emperor contemplated ways he could kill John even though there were rumors that John could not die until Jesus came back for the Church. He could have beheaded him but that form of execution was for Roman citizens. He could have fed him to the lions; however, the lions don't always eat Christians. After much contemplating, considering, envisioning, and envisaging, he and his servants came up with the idea of boiling John to death.

They boiled the oil in a cauldron over an open flame. The crowd chanted and cheered because they were about to witness the execution of the last Apostle. All the other Apostles were killed as many as thirty years earlier.

The herald decreed that John would boil in oil and the proceedings began. John was softly praying when they lowered him in the hot cauldron. The evil emperor watched in anticipation but was disappointed because John was still praying in the hot oil. The roaring crowd began to settle as they watched John in prayer. Then he raised his hands and began praising God in his trial, in his tribulation, in his circumstance and the emperor became angry, he was fuming and livid, he was irate and just plain mad. Instead of destroying faith in Christ Jesus, it was increased. I would almost bet Emperor Domitian was as red as a beet. Since the emperor could not kill the beloved Apostle, he had him exiled at the Isle of Patmos. John lived there with the Lord and wrote his Gospel of Jesus Christ according to John and three other epistles. Also while in exile, he took dictation and wrote *The Revelation of Jesus Christ*. John lived on the island for two years. The ban was lifted when Emperor Domitian died and John's banishment was lifted. He lived out his days as the Pastor in Ephesus until he died in his sleep.

In Closing

Satan has been attempting to eliminate the Church since its inception. He influenced Herod in an attempt to kill Jesus when He was just two years old. He personally tried again 28 years later in the wilderness and came up wanting. Had he known His death at the cross would bring salvation and freedom to all who accept Christ, he would have fought tooth and nail to cancel the His crucifixion. If he had known the power the believers in Christ would receive, he would have stopped the trial. He couldn't stop God's plan with Jesus giving His life so men and women would live to make up the Church or the body of Christ.

Now his focus is on the Church or the believers around the world. He has many conspirators at his deposal day in and day out who also attempt discourage believers, however, if he can't discourage believers, he will attempt to influence people to create a heretic gospel, or a shadow of the Gospel of Jesus Christ.

The Church or the body of Jesus the Christ, Jesus the Messiah is designed by God to be His power on the earth. Our power is to overcome evil and witness to the world as sons and daughters of light. Satan desires to pollute the Church by the flesh and he has been doing damage to the Church for years. Spiritual warfare is not only in the world but also in the Church. He is influencing men and women ministers who are not called by God to pastor churches around the world. The evidence of this is simply, "no power but chaos in their church."

An example is the Catholic Church. Most Catholic churches pray to Mary as mother of God instead of Jesus, Son of God. There is no power in that prayer because it is prayed to the wrong address. The results of this are wayward priest fondling and molesting children in the church instead of teaching the ways of Christ. Furthermore, it blinds the congregation to cater to the flesh with abominations such as gay marriages. Catholics are not the only one and all Catholics are not corrupt in Scriptures. However, they do have a tendency to get off track as they did a few centuries ago when the commoners/congregation paid the church to transfer their dead relatives from hell to Heaven. There are other church leaders who operate in a fleshly orientation which is not spiritually healthy. We have leaders in churches that pay their rent, car notes, insurance, and utilities secretly from the church's bank account. Then there are those who make up doctrine every week to please the congregation in order to collect money. These activities are simply Satan's influence on these particular leaders. In these last days, it will be these leaders that disrespect God's ordinances today, and will come against true believers to do bodily harm later.

The men and women of God's true Church are to be sober-minded in all things. We have to be in tune with God because Satan is constantly looking for someone to devour, someone meandering through life with a title, or position in the Church. He will use a babe in Christ to spread gossip just as fast as using a Teacher of the Gospel with a wandering eye. He will use offense and unforgiveness wherever he can and millions of people will fall for it.

If the Church wants to successful, we have to ward off all things in the flesh and stick with the principals of God. We have to be true to the Scriptures and let the Scriptures bring truth to us and through us. The Church needs to live and breathe God's Word everyday of the week and not just on Sundays and Wednesdays. We have to be still and allow God to bring Pastors, Teachers, Praise Leaders and Deacons into the Church and qualify them through Timothy and Titus instead of nepotism, or cliques or the good ol' boy system.

As we discovered in the last chapter, this Gospel can kill you as it caused the death of the eleven. Satan's church, (unbelievers), is sharpening their swords and their tongues to devour, consume, demolish, and overcome true believers. The Body of Christ cannot afford to be slacking, napping or coasting – especially in these times, because coasting is another form of backsliding. As the ten virgins were encouraged to be ready, Jesus encourages us to watch and pray. Remember only five of the virgins were ready and five were not. This may be an indication that only half the Church will go with Jesus to glory while the rest are left behind. We cannot afford to be lazy like the lazy servant who buried his mina, or the busy ones who have the need to inspect their property instead of fellowshipping with God.

We, as the Body of Christ need to shake off the traditions of men because it does not allow God to work freely with His children. In fact, the tradition of men handcuffs God and renders Him helpless to help the Church, because the Church is helping herself with personalized rules and contrary interpretations. We cannot afford to make up rules as we go along and call ourselves blessed. We cannot afford to vote on what God says in the Bible and be a thriving and powerful Church in Word and deed. We cannot afford to try to live under the Law and under Grace at the same time and call ourselves blessed. We cannot allow people in the Church who don't qualify to be leaders according to the blueprint set in *Timothy* and *Titus*. We need to know that some are called, some are sent, and some just went.

The Church will be under attack in the last days and God will allow it. He will give Satan permission to assault the believers and many of us will die and join the martyrs in *Revelation 6:9*. However, if we are not walking in the light as He is the Light, we will join the rest of the nonbelievers in the lake of fire and brimstone.

Notes:

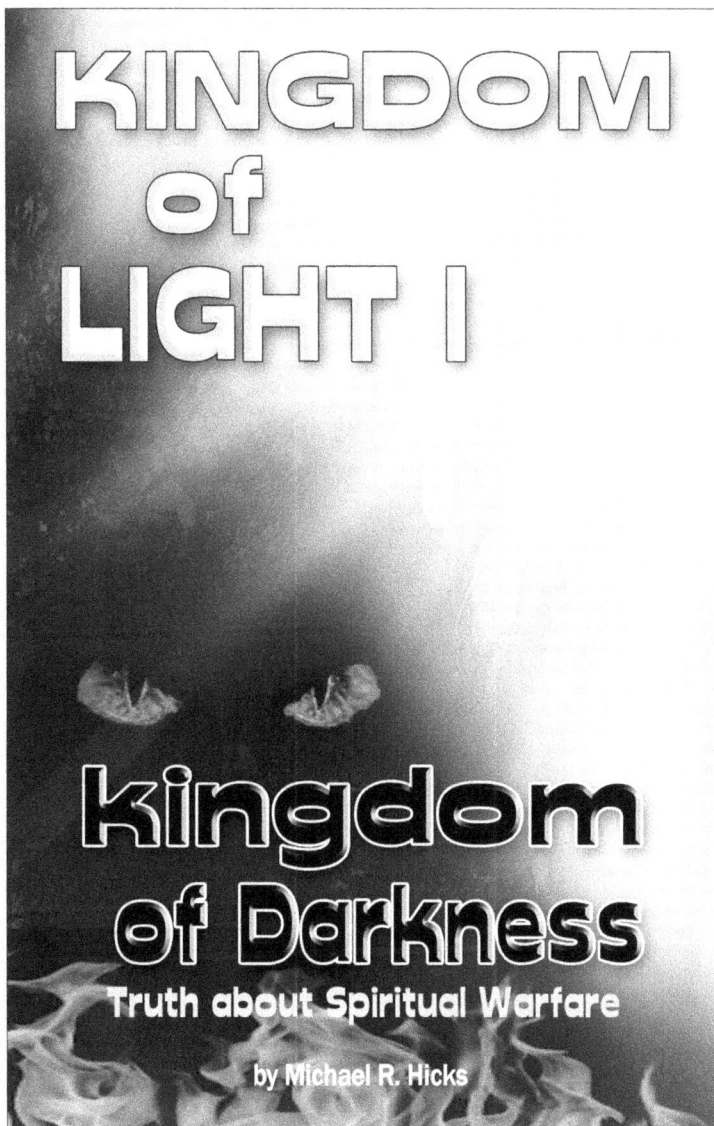

Restore your DREAMS   Reignite your PRAYERS
See your VISION completed!

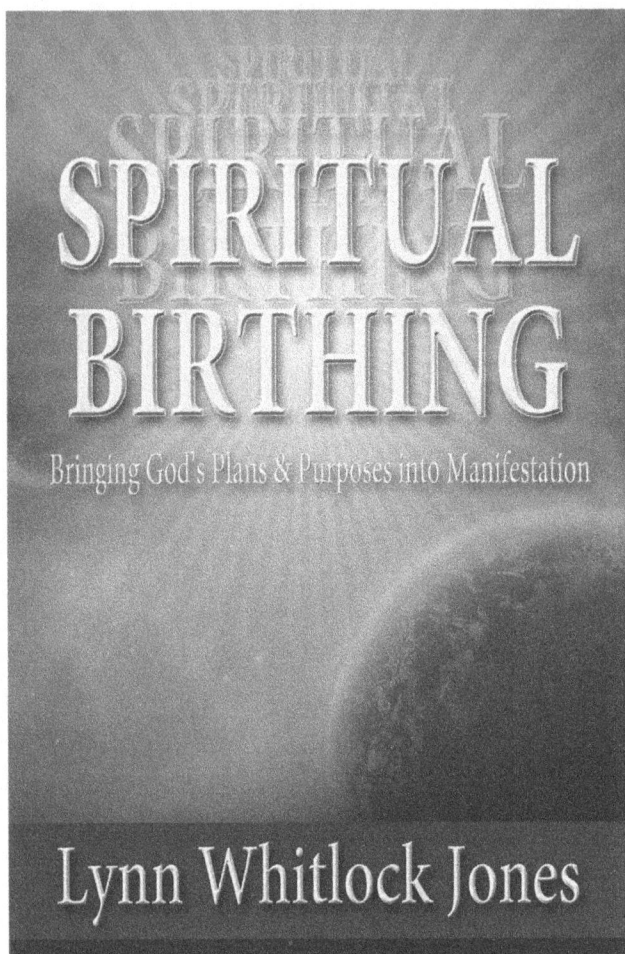

"As the message of this book sinks into your spirit, may you be moved into action. Lynn has used first hand experience not second hand knowledge, to put this book together. Time to launch out!" -- *David Knox*

Pastor/Missionary
Grove Christian Center

Available at select Bookstores and
www.boldtruthpublishing.com